Cambridge IGCSE ®

India Studies

Nigel Price ▶ Anjali Tyagi

Nicholas R. Fellows ▶ Mike Wells

CAMBRIDGE
UNIVERSITY PRESS

CAMBRIDGE
UNIVERSITY PRESS

University Printing House, Cambridge CB2 8BS, United Kingdom

Cambridge University Press is part of the University of Cambridge.

It furthers the University's mission by disseminating knowledge in the pursuit of
education, learning and research at the highest international levels of excellence.

www.cambridge.org
Information on this title: www.cambridge.org/9780521149235

© Cambridge University Press 2013

First published 2013

A catalogue record for this publication is available from the British Library

ISBN 978-0-521-14923-5 Paperback

Contents

Preface

India is on its way to becoming one of the great powers of the twenty-first century. Cambridge *IGCSE India Studies* offers you the chance to understand the dynamic rise of this new superpower. The syllabus investigates a series of themes and case studies aimed at exploring what drives modern India. In the process, you learn to analyse problems, recognise alternative perspectives and make reasoned judgements.

Armed with these skills, Cambridge *IGCSE India Studies* will show you how to make sense of emerging India and judge the achievements, challenges and opportunities facing the world's largest democracy. The syllabus builds on existing good practice in international education and current thinking in area studies to provide a lively and innovative trans-disciplinary course.

This textbook has been written to support Paper 1 of the syllabus. Each unit is dedicated to the four themes identified in the syllabus, examining the core issues that underpin it:

- Sustaining Indian Democracy
- Economic Development
- Social and Cultural Development
- India and the World.

For each theme, the syllabus sets out four key issues. Every key issue is a question that shapes the structure of this book, making every chapter an enquiry investigating its theme and issues in three ways:

- Why is India changing?
- How far and fast is India changing?
- How are these changes affecting India?

Each unit begins by outlining the aims as well as the key concepts which will be discussed. This is followed with a timeline that lists major events you ought to know. Next, a brief introduction is provided so as to help you understand the context in which the ensuing chapters are set.

Every chapter begins with a key question that helps you to focus on thinking about the theme as a critical enquiry. The coverage of key issues in each theme guarantees that you cover the syllabus. In addition, chapters are supported by maps, figures and images as well as elements such as activities, 'Aid to Learning' questions and 'Focus' fact boxes. All these are meant to help you to understand and evaluate the concept. There are also several case studies which dig into important events and ideas, setting you a problem to think about. There are also end-of-the-chapter exercises that improve your exam skills and allow your study to be focused.

Cambridge *IGCSE India Studies* wants you to take a critical approach to every topic as it takes a broad view, drawing on a range of disciplines to offer enquiry into and reflection on the challenges and opportunities (local, regional, national and international) facing India today. Cambridge *IGCSE India Studies* will help you to develop a wide range of skills and ways of thinking that active citizens of the future will need. By investigating topics from different perspectives you will develop a global outlook along with skills in enquiry and independent thinking.

Unit 1

Sustaining Indian Democracy

Aims of the Unit

- Understand the political processes of India since 1989
- Evaluate the different meanings of the word 'people' in the Indian context
- Analyse how India's diversity and plural party politics have affected democracy
- Explain the nature of India as a nation as laid down in the Constitution
- Get a clear picture of the political structures and substructures prevalent in India
- Understand the concepts of nationalism and secularism and their changing connotations in the present day India
- Recognise the symbiotic relation between political parties and caste groups
- Evaluate the election process in India and how electoral practices threaten the democracy
- Examine critically India's general elections from 1989

Key Concepts

Democracy: Government of, by and for the people who vote for their own elected representatives

Sustaining democracy: The survival and success of the Indian Democratic Federal Republic, the world's largest and liveliest democracy

Plural party politics: Political parties making alliances with other parties to work together to form stable governments or effective oppositions

Nationalism: The political, social, religious and ethnic influences that helped to create India as an independent nation state and sustain it now

Castes: Social classes of hereditary groups, separated into *jatis* (castes), and made up of a wide range of clans or *gotras*. Discrimination on grounds of caste is illegal under the Constitution of India

Secularism: Not having things (such as the state, school etc.) controlled by a religion or religions; Politics free of religious influence so that religious philosophies do not influence policies

Communalism: Encouraging mistrust and violence between the different racial and religious communities such as Hindu, Muslim, Sikh and Christian. Caste politics have a powerful influence over the general governance of a country like India

Sovereign: Having a free government not controlled by any foreign power

Socialism: Having social and economic equality under state ownership and control

Secular: Not controlled or influenced by any religion or religious group or ideas

Republic: A state where the Head of State is elected by the people and is not monarchical

Fraternity: A group of people or a community united by common purposes, interests and tastes

Time Line

1989 – National Front Government (led by Janata Dal)

1991 – Congress (I) Government (led by Narashima Rao)

1996 – United Front Government (First Bharatiya Janata Party Government: 16 to 31 March)

1996 – United Front Government (led by Janata Dal)

1998 – National Democratic Alliance (Second BJP Government: March 1998 to October 1999)

1999 – National Democratic Alliance (Third BJP Government)

2004 – United Progressive Alliance (led by Indian National Congress Party)

2009 – United Progressive Alliance (led by Indian National Congress Party)

The Indian Constitution

The Indian political system is founded on a written constitution, overseen by the Parliament, dependent upon a democratic electoral system involving political parties. The Indian Constitution came into force on 26 January, 1950. All the twenty-eight states and the seven union territories constituting India are subject to it. Its formation was the first step to a parliamentary form of governance.

The constitution was written by a drafting committee chaired by Dr B. R. Ambedkar. Influential committee members, including Jawaharlal Nehru, represented the West-oriented, English-speaking, upper class Indian elite.

The British Westminster Parliamentary Government system was accepted, creating a multi-party democracy that makes all registered adults above the age of eighteen eligible to vote.

The Visions of the Constitution

The Constitution provides for a parliamentary form of government which is federal in structure with certain unitary features. The Constitution can be described broadly in terms of the following key facts.

- It is a written document with specific articles and schedules.
- It contains clear statements outlining how institutions are to be established.
- Procedures are there for amendments to be made to address changing social and political developments.
- It embodies a precise and detailed description of India, the nation.

The 'Founding Fathers' of the Constitution wanted a new and independent India. So they described India as a Sovereign, Democratic Republic, with 'Socialist' and 'Secular' added later via amendments (see Fig 1.1).

PREAMBLE

WE THE PEOPLE OF INDIA having solemnly
resolved to constitute India into a SOVEREIGN
SOCIALIST SECULAR DEMOCRATIC REPUBLIC
and to secure to all its citizens:

JUSTICE, social, economic and political;
LIBERTY of thought, expression, belief, faith and worship;
EQUALITY of status and of opportunity;
and to prompt among them all
FRATERNITY assuming the dignity of individual and
the unity and integrity of the Nation;

IN OUR CONSTITUENT ASSEMBLY the twenty-sixth
day of November, 1949, do, HEREBY ADOPT,
ENACT AND GIVE TO OURSERVES THIS CONSTITUTION.

Fig. 1.1 Preamble to the Indian Constitution

Aid to Learning

1. Which aspects of the Indian Constitution do you think might create problems for sustaining democracy?
2. Why did the Congress Party not lead India after the November 1989 general election?

Activities

1. In groups of three or four discuss which of the key words, other than 'democratic', are the most essential as far as democracy in India is concerned. The group needs to reach a consensus about it.
2. The group can then organise all the key words in the order of priority and justify the sequence.
3. One representative from each group can present the group's decisions before the class and ask for the views of the class on them.

Words of Advice

The above activities will help you engage with the views of others as well as enable you to get your own views across to others. It will improve your thinking, listening, reasoning and judging skills.

The President

The President is the 'First Citizen', the Commander in Chief of the Armed Forces and the Constitutional Head of the Executive of the Union. The President and Vice President are elected by the members of the Electoral College. The Electoral College is made up of the elected members of the Lok Sabha and the Rajya Sabha as well as those of the Legislative Assembly of each state and union territory.

The President is responsible for making a wide variety of appointments such as Governors of States, the Chief Justice, other judges of the Supreme Court and High Courts of India, the Attorney General, Comptroller and Auditor General as well as Chief Election Commissioner.

Rajya Sabha and Lok Sabha

The political system allows many political parties to sit in the two chambers of the Parliament. The Upper House is called Rajya Sabha. This Council of States has 250 representatives serving for six years with elections taking place every two years. 228 are elected indirectly by legislatures of each state and union territory, with a further 12 nominated by the President. The Upper House reviews and revises bills and settles conflicts over legislation.

Fig. 1.2 The Rajya Sabha Chamber (The Upper House)

The House of the People is called the Lok Sabha. 543 representatives are elected every five years at the Lok Sabha. Representatives have to be at least 25 years of age. Members of the Lok Sabha come from the different states and union territories. This number varies from state to state, depending on the population, from 80 from Uttar Pradesh to 1 from Nagaland. The Lok Sabha questions ministers, makes resolutions, oversees administration and safeguards people's rights. The Lok Sabha also discusses economic and social planning, social welfare, inflation and price control. Laws can be made from the Union List. Subjects dealt with include foreign affairs, defence, transport and communications, currency and taxation.

Fig. 1.3 The Lok Sabha Chamber (The Lower House)

The Prime Minister

The Prime Minister as Head of the Government, together with the senior cabinet ministers and the ministers of State, lead the council of ministers. The Prime Minister advises the President over the appointment of cabinet ministers. The Prime Minister along with the Council have come to be the real 'power house', controlling maximum executive authority. The office of the Prime Minister is the 'nerve centre' of all executive decisions, supported by the Cabinet Secretariat.

Activities

Imagine the new Chinese ambassador to India is to visit your school as part of a cultural tour of your region. Your principal has been asked to chair a 'Question and Answer' session, with the questions being provided by your class showing how India's parliamentary system works and what it is responsible for. Your principal has asked your class to prepare a special presentation.

1. In small groups, consider why each of the four bullet points below is important to modern India.
   - Parliamentary democracy
   - Responsibilities of the Upper and Lower Houses of Parliament
   - The work of the government of the day
   - The way laws are made
2. Each group should then prepare a short presentation explaining the importance of each for India today. Your presentation should not last longer than three minutes.
3. Your teacher will then judge each group's efforts and score each presentation out of 10. You will be further graded by each of the other groups on a scale of ten. The group with the highest score from the class and the teacher will lead the 'Question and Answer' session with the important visitor.

India's Electoral System

India is described as a democracy in the Constitution. This requires free and fair elections to be conducted in order to have a body of elected representatives to govern the country. The principle of 'Universal Adult Suffrage' governs voting. The National Parliamentary Elections are decided by a 'First Past the Post' system, i.e. an election won in each constituency by the candidate with the most votes. Turn-out at elections has been approximately 58 per cent on an average.

Table 1.1   Voting percentages through the years

Year	Percentage
1989	61.95%
1991	56.93%
1996	57.94%
1998	61.97%
1999	59.99%
2004	48.74%
2009	59.7%

Voting is carried out by 'secret ballot'. The voters need to register on the electoral roll which is updated every year. These days voting is conducted electronically using Electronic Voting Machines (EVM). The voters are required to cast their votes in person.

Aid to Learning

1. Explain what the following mean.
    (a) First Past the Post
    (b) Electoral Roll
    (c) Secret Ballot

The Political Parties of India

The Indian Constitution allows a multi-party system to develop within a federal structure. The national parties offer their candidature to form the Central Government in New Delhi. The regional parties focus predominantly on forming the State Governments. A party has national recognition if there has been evidence of its success, established status and representation in several states. Currently, there are seven 'recognised' national parties.

The regional parties participate in various elections but only within their state. To be recognised as a state party and hence to be granted a unique party symbol, an organisation must have a certain percentage of votes or seats. Examples of state parties are the Shiv Sena (Maharashtra), the Telugu Desam Party (Andhra Pradesh), the Akali Dal (Punjab) and the All India Anna Dravida Munnetra Kazagham (Tamil Nadu).

Parties have also developed through the strong leadership of one important individual. For example, Indira Gandhi exercised full control over her Congress Party (Indira) in the 1970s. Similarly, Bal Thackeray dominated the Shiv Sena Party during his lifetime.

Caste Politics in India

The Government of India has endorsed a reservation system for education and jobs in an attempt to redress caste discrimination identified by the Mandal Commission in 1979–80. It was introduced by the V.P. Singh Government in 1989. The reservation system operates by setting quotas corresponding to the castes included in the official list. Castes, so favoured, have the opportunity to apply for reserved places in education, employment and training.

However, the reservation system has not been received well by all. Castes not included in the list, termed as 'forward castes', dislike it because they think it creates reverse discrimination and is basically unfair. Other critics of the reservation system have argued that appointments should be based on the personal merit of each individual.

The Political Parties and the Castes

Garnering and using the votes of caste-groups have been of great interest to many political parties. It has been termed 'vote bank politics', the aim of which has been to gain electoral support from the backward classes. Given below are examples of political parties linked directly with certain specific caste-groups.

The Bahujan Samaj Party and Kanshi Ram

Kanshi Ram, born a Dalit in Punjab, formed the Bahujan Samaj Party (BSP) in 1984. He had been a government employee until the mid-1960s. In 1978, he set up the All-India Backward and Minority Communities Employees Federation (BAMCEF). Ram's importance to the BSP stemmed from his influential position in the leather workers' sub-caste known as 'Dalit Chamar' in North India. The BSP won 67 seats in the 1993 state elections in Uttar Pradesh. It also had an impact on the Madhya Pradesh State Legislature by increasing its seats to twelve which was an impressive six fold rise.

By 1995, BSP had left the State Government of Uttar Pradesh and entered into an alliance with the BJP. BJP had gone out of its way to sponsor Dalit and OBC leaders. This was a strategic move, meant to endorse its anti-elitist and anti-upper-class affinities.

The BSP formed a new government with the Dalit-born Mayawati as the Chief Minister of Uttar Pradesh. Mayawati held this office in 1995, in 1997 and from May 2002 to August 2003. From May 2007 she remained in office until 2012. Her main agenda has focussed on social justice for the weaker sections of Uttar Pradesh with policies designed to increase employment. Addressing corruption, especially in the police departments, has been another important issue on Mayawati's agenda.

The Samajwadi Party and Mulayam Singh Yadav

In Uttar Pradash, the Samajwadi Party (SP), under the leadership of Mulayam Singh Yadav, won the 1993 state elections. It was one of the greatest rivals of the BSP. To accomplish this victory, the SP had sought the alliance of the 'backward classes', the members of the minority such as the Muslims and the members of the Yadava caste to which Mulayam Singh himself belonged. This, in turn, culminated in a coalition government with the Dalit-supported BSP.

In the 2004 national elections, the SP ended up as the fourth largest party in the Lok Sabha with 36 of the 38 members from Uttar Pradesh. At the national level, the SP gave external support to the Manmohan Singh Minority Government. The SP also entered into an alliance with the smaller Rashtriya Lok Dal Party, led by Chaudhary Ajit Singh. The 2007 Uttar Pradesh state elections having resulted in a loss of seats, Yadav resigned to allow Mayawati to resume the office of Chief Minister. In the 2009 general elections, SP gained only 23 seats despite an alliance with Rashtriya Janta Dal (RJD), led by Lalu Prasad Yadav. It is currently the third largest party in the Parliament.

Dalit Leader Udit Raj

More and more Dalit leaders came to realise that their interests should be represented as a case apart from that of those classified as OBC. An example of one such leader is Udit Raj. Raj founded the Justice Party (JP) which is officially known as the South Indian Liberal Federation and is a former Dravidian political party. Raj was born into a backward caste in Uttar Pradesh. Throughout its history, the JP has campaigned against the plight of the backward classes. It has, often controversially, opposed Brahmin involvement in the Civil Service and politics, rejecting the views of Gandhi and focussing on caste based reservations, especially for Dalits.

Aid to Learning

1. "The Constitution's vision of India being a Democratic Republic was more important than India being a 'Sovereign, Socialist or Secular state.'" How far do you agree?" Give reasons for your answer.

2. What view do you personally take of the reservation system? Or are you more in favour of appointments being governed by personal merit? Have a class discussion.

3. To what extent do you think caste based parties have succeeded in improving the condition of the Dalits and the other backward classes? Have a class discussion.

   The following websites will help you with the above tasks.

   www.ideasforindia.in/article.aspx?article_id=81articles.timesofindia.indiatimes.com/2011-07-27/india/29820335

   www.dalitnetwork.org

Chapter 1 — Democracy by Coalition

Key Question

Does Indian democracy benefit from coalitions and plural party politics?

Introduction

The word 'democracy' is derived from the Greek *demokratia* (coined from *demos* meaning 'people' and *kratos* meaning 'rule'). Democracy can be simply understood as 'people's rule'. However, when you look at actual situations you might not find it as simple. When we say 'people's rule', which people do we mean? Does it mean all the people of a country regardless of differences in caste, class, religion or gender? Yet all the people of a country do not agree about everything related to the governance and politics of the country. Such a thing is not possible among people whose customs, cultures, beliefs and habits are as diverse as in India. So, any discussion on democracy in India needs to take into account the different meanings of the word 'people' itself. In this light, we can explore and determine the various facets of democracy in India.

Led by many governments and influential leaders, India has developed at a steady pace, eventually becoming a world power with the capacity for rapid economic growth. Coalition governments are more consensus-based, resulting in policies which better represent the electorate's wishes, are of a better quality and are subject to enhanced scrutiny and attention. Coalition governance also prevents rule by any one particular group. A large section of India's population has benefited from the rapid progress and development in recent years. At the same time, millions of disadvantaged people still live on less than $1 a day.

The topics discussed in this chapter allow you to take a critical and analytical view of coalition politics in modern democratic India.

The Janata Dal led Coalition of 1989–1990

Review of Indian Politics in 1989

No single political party had been able to form a majority government despite the fact that the Congress Party could no longer control matters on its own. The coalition led by Janata Dal came to power after the 1989 general elections.

Nehru and his family supporters had consistently insisted on promoting a 'socialist' democracy. Their influence, however, had declined as had the power of long established political leaders who had previously held much control over their parties and political activities.

More and more parties started to compete for power. Many parties began to support regional interests, to further the Hindu cause and to promote the issues affecting discriminated groups in Indian society. Parties also campaigned to attract the support of the millions of 'caste voters'.

Aid to Learning

What do these words/phrases mean? Explain them in a few words of your own.

(a) Family dynasty

(b) Party hierarchies

(c) Marginalised groups

(d) Caste voters

(e) Coalition

The Decline of Congress Party Control

The loss of control or power of the Congress Party was neither sudden nor entirely unexpected. The ground for its decline had already been prepared by a number of factors. Some of them are given below.

1. People's aspirations and attitudes to the long-established monopoly of the Congress Party were changing. The 1967 general elections saw Congress win only 40 per cent of the Lok Sabha seats. Previously, Congress had always retained up to 70 per cent of seats in the Assembly elections.

2. There developed a crisis over who was to become Prime Minister, Indira Gandhi or Morarji Desai. Indira Gandhi won.

3. Indira Gandhi's feeling for the need to be assertive after the election defeats made her very unpopular with senior colleagues, who expelled her from the party for 'ill-discipline' in November 1969, thereby splitting the Congress Party into Congress (O) led by Desai and Congress (I) led by Indira Gandhi.

4. In 1975, the then President declared an 'Emergency' on Indira Gandhi's request so as to end the resistance to her staying in office. Main opponents were arrested, civil liberty restrictions were made, censorship of the press increased and more powers were given to the Prime Minister. All this made voters in certain regions hostile towards the Congress (I) Party and created dissatisfaction among the voters in general.

5. The 'backward classes' were constantly demanding more recognition and concrete redress of their grievances, while often feeling ignored.

The Results of the General Elections, November 1989

The 'National Front' led by Janata Dal won the 1989 general elections, supported by the 'left' and the 'right wing' parties. The JD Coalition took over, bringing the 'One-Party' dominance of Congress to an end. In many ways the 9th Lok Sabha Elections were a watershed moment in Indian electoral politics.

Table 1.2   Results of the November 1989 General Elections

Party	No. of Seats	Votes Polled %
Congress	197	39.5
CPI	12	2.6
CPI (M)	33	6.6
BJP	86	11.4
JD	142	17.8
Total	543	62.0 (turnout)

Communist Party of India (CPI), Communist Party of India (Marxist) (CPI (M)), Jana Sangh/Bharatiya Janata Party (BJP), Janata Dal (JD)

Aid to Learning

Look at **Table 1.2** and answer the following questions briefly.

1. How many seats would Janata Dal need to be able to form a government?
2. Find out how many seats the coalition parties collectively held? (For example, do an internet search).
3. What is meant by the term 'turnout'?

The Political Parties of the 'Clutch' Government

Four competing political parties took the opportunity to gain power in 1989. The 'National Front' coalition created by Janata Dal took office, led by V.P. Singh, supported by BJP, which was a Hindu nationalist party, and the Communist Parties — CPI and CPI (M). This was not a strong alliance, with political leaders constantly at odds with each other. To understand the reasons behind this, we need to look into the history of each party.

The Janata Dal

The Janata Dal Party, founded in 1988 by Raja Vishwanath Pratap Singh, saw itself as an India 'Centre-Left' Coalition. It was supported by opposing factions of the Janata Dal Party and the Bharatiya Lok Dal (BLD), which was formed at the end of 1974 through the alliance of seven parties opposed to the autocratic rule of Indira Gandhi.

In 1977, the BLD combined with the Jan Sangh and the Indian National Congress (O) to form the Janata Party, with its main support coming from the 'lower' caste agricultural peasantry. The party opposed the authoritarian and allegedly 'corrupt' Congress (I) Government, arguing for improvement of the basic daily needs of its supporters and an end to the discrimination against the 'lower' castes.

Communist Party of India (CPI)

The CPI emerged as a combination of Communist Parties and 'Leftist' strands (the 'Left Front'). The main aim of the CPI policies concentrated on huge public sector spending on social and economic needs of the masses. The party defends secular policies, national integrity, rights for workers, minorities, tribal groups, Dalits and other deprived sections.

The party visualised economic development in the form of land reforms, fair wages to agricultural-workers, gender justice, education to all and social security and health care for each and every citizen. It pledged that the future of India rested on a separate and independent foreign policy. The party advocated 'Marxism' as its underlying philosophy.

Communist Party of India (Marxist)

The CPI(M) was founded in 1964. The party's political views were basically the same as those of the CPI, but with an emphasis on scientific Marxist-Leninist analysis to carry forward its revolutionary tasks and mobilise all the exploited sections of the Indian people in order to operate on the principle of democratic centralism. The Party's aim focussed on socialism and communism through the establishment of the state of a 'dictatorship of the proletariat', acting on behalf of the workers.

Bharatiya Janata Party

The BJP was formed in 1980 by A.B. Vajpayee and L.K. Advani, leaders who believed that this new 'Centre-Right', Hindu nationalist party should represent most Indians. The party's manifesto highlights conservative social programmes and encouragement of economic growth. 'Self-reliance' was established as the core of the party's values. The BJP has committed itself to work towards creating a modern, powerful, prosperous, progressive and secure India.

Aid to Learning

1. Find out why the new 1989 Government was called the 'Clutch' Government.
2. What are the fundamental differences between the ideologies of the political parties involved in the 'Clutch' Government?

A Difficult Start for the Coalition

Once in power, the government found it difficult to introduce its coalition programmes. The Singh administration hoped to follow policies which would assist the needs of the backward castes and put an end to caste-based discrimination. However, all new policies had to wait as violence and insurgency erupted in Punjab, Assam and Kashmir. Relations with the Sikh community were very low after the controversial Operation Blue Star in 1984.

Fig. 1.4 Akal Takht building after Operation Blue Star

At the same time, militant groups in Assam demanded to be independent, reacting to what they saw as a 'take-over' by non-Assamese immigrants in business, industry and government sectors. The Indian Army carried out a series of assaults and the government brought in procedures for Assam residents to become much more a part of the political set-up in the region. Even so, 'tribal' groups from the north of Assam continued armed attacks against the police and the military.

Meanwhile, insurgency in Kashmir continued as well. Violence of Islamic militant groups forced more than 100 000 Hindus to flee the Kashmir Valley. Hindu leaders wanted to preserve the culture of Kashmir and continue strong links with India. The Indian government was insistent that Kashmir was not to be granted 'autonomy', especially because of Pakistan's claims over the state.

So the Government increased the number of security forces to combat major insurgent groups. The more prominent of the insurgent groups were the secular, pro-independence Jammu and Kashmir Liberation Front (JKLF) and the Islamic and pro-Pakistani groups such as Hizbul Mujahideen (HUM) and Harkat-ul-Ansar. By 1996, at least 15 000–20 000 insurgents, police, paramilitary personnel, and civilians had lost their lives.

Reservation Policy of the Coalition

The Janata Dal Government believed that the backward classes needed government support to improve their lives. In 1989, the decision was made to implement the 1980 Mandal Commission Report. This report recommended that positions in certain types of employment (within Federal Government, public sector positions and some higher education posts) should be reserved for the 'Other Backward Classes' (OBCs), who represented about half of India's population. At the time, only 2 per cent of the Indian Administrative Service posts were given to OBCs. Government policy now stated that this percentage should be increased to 49.5 per cent. Many of India's upper castes strongly opposed what seemed to be a challenge to their age-old social position. They believed that they were being unjustly discriminated against and insisted that 'reserved' posts should be based on merit and ability.

Critics argued that it is unfair to accord people special privileges on the basis of caste. They also argued that unqualified candidates would assume important positions in society and be unable to go a good job. The result was demonstrations, violence and outright disobedience of the authorities. In September 1990, New Delhi came to a halt. Student demonstrations flared up; incidents of upper caste students setting themselves on fire became world news. In other parts of northern India, upper caste groups fought openly with people from the backward castes.

The Downfall of the Janata Dal Government

The collapse of the JD-led Coalition was due to four possible causes.

1. **Demands for Regional Separation**
   The JD-led Coalition had managed to resolve most of the political difficulties in Punjab and Assam. It was in Kashmir, however, that the situation escalated and insurgency broke out. The Indian Army engaged the extremists, but without any permanent success. The government was forced to increase its forces there. No peaceful settlement was reached.

2. **The Mandal Crisis**
   The bitter condemnation of government policy was too much for one of the Coalition partners. The BJP was concerned that full implementation of reservations would offend its upper-caste Hindu supporters. The party's official reason for leaving the Coalition was that the reservation policy was deeply flawed and would cause unwarranted social divisions.

3. **The Ayodhya Factor**

The 1986 edition of Encyclopædia Britannica reported that 'Sri Rama's birthplace is marked by a mosque, erected by the Mughal Emperor Babur in 1528 on the site of an earlier temple'. According to popular belief, the ancient temple had been destroyed on the orders of the Mughal Emperor. BJP was keen to see the birthplace of Lord Rama enshrined in a new temple. The demand for this new temple had been encouraged by the World Hindu Council (Viswa Hindu Parishad).

In September 1990, L.K. Advani undertook a *rath yatra* (pilgrimage on a chariot) from Somnath in Gujarat to Ayodhya. The purpose of this was to press for the establishment of the Ram Temple at Ayodhya where the Babri Masjid stood. BJP used the whole idea of Lord Rama as the symbol of a 'national' birthplace and 'national honour' to enhance the Party's support of Hindu nationalism. Regardless of whether BJP planned it or not, this could only bring its leaders into conflict with the coalition government, especially over the position and treatment of Muslims in Indian society. In 1992, a mob destroyed the old mosque. Who was responsible for the incident remains highly controversial.

4. **Continuing Tension and Unrest**

Tension and violence, particularly against the Muslim community, had become a feature of the 1980s. The following incidents give some evidence as to the difficulties the Janata Dal Government inherited.

(a) Hindu-Muslim riots had peaked in 1989, especially in the town of Bhagalpur, in Bihar. Over 1000 people were killed and 40 000 fled the region. Evidence was produced to show that the local authorities in Bihar had not really intervened.

(b) Hindus had objected to Muslims being granted their own Civil Code which allowed, for example, marriage to more than one wife.

(c) The situation in Kashmir, exploited by Muslim extremists, had created further fear. The continued insurgency, in the eyes of many, might result in the separation of the region from India.

(d) By the end of the 1980s, (anti-Muslim) Hindu women had become popular political activists. At the height of the glorification of Lord Rama at Ayodhya, Uma Bharati and Sadhvi Rithambara addressed huge crowds urging outright violence against Muslims in support of 'National Hinduism.'

The Importance of the Janata Dal Government

The government led by Janata Dal lasted just over a year and its attempt to survive a very difficult time revealed serious problems that all future government coalitions would face while delivering their set programmes. Governments would always face strong 'Official Opposition'. A coalition government would need to develop strategies and policies that would not offend its 'co-partners in power'. A stable government would need to accommodate the political beliefs of its coalition partners. It would only take one sensitive issue for a coalition government to struggle and for splits to take place.

Main Coalition Governments since 1990

The Narasimha Rao Government

Narasimha Rao became Prime Minister after the collapse of Janta Dal Government and led a stable 'minority government' for five years. He was brought out of retirement to lead the Congress Party following the assassination of Rajiv Gandhi during the election campaign. A low vote of 53 per cent gave Congress 244 seats, with the second party, BJP, led by Advani, winning 120 seats; Janata Dal Party became the third party with 59 seats, led by V.P. Singh.

Rao's term as Prime Minister was an eventful one. The problems that the Singh (1989–1990) Government had been facing continued. The Rao Government was challenged by insurgency, terrorism, Hindu-Muslim riots, motions of 'No Confidence' and allegations of corruption. Yet, the administration was responsible for liberalising the economy with greater freedom of trade and for preparing the ground for growth. Overseas investment was heavily encouraged, together with reforms of the financial systems.

A 'Look East' foreign policy was developed and relations were also cultivated with Iran and Israel. USA, UK and other western powers were invited to assist in promoting security measures against terrorism. The Rao Government never gave in to terrorist demands. By 1995, a nuclear programme had been planned ready for implementation.

The Rao Government successfully checked the separatist movement in Northern Punjab, rejecting their demand for independence. It introduced the Terrorist and Disruptive Activities (Prevention) Act (TADA). It was India's first anti-terrorism legislation. The government also directed the Indian Army to eliminate the infiltrators. The law gave wide-ranging powers to law enforcement agencies for dealing with terrorist and 'socially disruptive' activities. However, there was a cost as tourism declined and special police units were often accused of committing atrocities against the local population.

The Minority Government faced claims that it no longer held enough support to continue in power. Rao and the other ministers were accused of bribing ten members of the Jharkhand Mukti Morcha Party (JMM) to vote for the Government to stay in power. Accusations were also made against Rao for forging documents in the St. Kitts Forgery Scandal.

Aid to Learning

1. What were the main problems that the Rao Government faced in 1990?
2. What were the Rao Government's main policies to improve the economy?
3. What action did the Rao Government take against terrorism?

The Bharatiya Janata Party Rule (1998–2004)

BJP came to power in 1998 with 182 seats, depending heavily on the support of the All India Anna Dravida Munnetra Kazagham (AIADMK) and its allies in the Samata Party, Shiromani Akali Dal and Shiv Sena. The coalition collapsed when Jayalaliltha, leader of the AIADMK, withdrew her support.

However, the BJP-led National Democratic Alliance won 303 seats in the 1999 general elections. This administration, led by Atal Bihari Vajpayee, lasted five years, making it the first Non-Congress government to last the full term in office.

Vajpayee's government sustained the Indian democratic system in three main ways.

1. It gave the voters a real choice between the main party alliances.
2. It halted the increasing break-up of the party system, despite regional, communal and caste differences (from 1989 to 1999, there had been five general elections and six Prime Ministers).
3. It continued the good practice of previous governments.

There were difficulties over economic problems, insurgency, terrorism and religious tensions. To make things worse, party rifts were always there in the background. The BJP continued to expand the liberalisation of the economy. Large government corporations were privatised and trade further opened up within World Trade Organisation rules. Commercial airlines were encouraged to fly to Indian cities. Private developers were allowed to rebuild cities and unrestricted overseas investment from multinational organisations was permitted. Despite terrorist attacks, the leadership of the BJP encouraged the build-up of closer relations with Pakistan. The Lahore Declaration was signed in 1999. In 2001, President Musharraf of Pakistan attended summit talks in Delhi. Although the talks broke down, the basis for future moves towards more peaceful co-operation had been set out.

The political and religious tensions of the early 1990s were also eased because once securely in power, the BJP did not want to prevent progress by openly supporting extreme Hindu nationalism, even though they had used the issue of building a Ram Temple at Ayodhya to get votes. Policies focussed more on the needs of the communities, with emphasis on improved anti-terror measures, education for all, agricultural reforms, etc. The government promoted nuclear power initiatives and nuclear tests, and focused on increasing bilateral ties with the US, UK and other Western Powers.

The First Manmohan Singh Government (2004–2009)

The BJP had gone for an early election, counting on rising regional and caste support and confident of defending their performance in government. However, Congress took over with 145 seats as against 138 seats won by the BJP. The India National Congress-led United Progressive Alliance formed an administration. But, Congress had only 27 per cent of the votes, and alliance with Communist Party supporters was going to test the strength of the UPA, particularly when the issue of nuclear power agreements came into play.

Prime Minister Manmohan Singh had been the inspiration behind the economic changes of the Rao administration. Economic reforms were continued in the banking and financial sectors as well as in the public sector corporations. A pro-industrialised economy was encouraged with a range of tax policies. The government created a 9 per cent economic growth rate — evidence of huge economic expansion. Debt relief policies to poor farmers were extended. On the other hand, the Singh Government was greatly criticised for not taking hold of the recent economic boom and diverting resources to reduce the widening gap between the rich and the poor.

Fig. 1.5   Manmohan Singh with the Chinese Premier, Wen Jiabao

The peace process with Pakistan carried on, attempting to continue the momentum gained earlier. Efforts were made to reduce terrorism and increase prosperity in Kashmir. The radical 'Students Islamic Movement of India' was banned. Relations with the Western Powers were also enhanced and the 'Look East' policy of the previous government was carried forward. Relations improved with Iran and Israel. India paid special attention to relations with Afghanistan, offering increased aid packages.

Pursuing relations with China was not easy. But steps forward became possible through the re-opening of the Nathula Pass in 2006 and Manmohan Singh's China visit in 2008. By 2007, China had become India's largest trading partner.

Much of the Singh Government's efforts were given to cementing Indo-US ties as well. India was determined to use the goodwill of President Bush to sign a nuclear agreement which would allow access to nuclear fuel and technologies. This came in 2008 but not without international debate, the greatest opponent being the CPI from within the UPA. But the Coalition Government just managed to survive the political crisis. In 2009, Manmohan Singh became the only Prime Minister since Jawaharlal Nehru to return to power after completing a full five year term. Policies in health, education and employment were extended and restructured. The National Rural Health Mission encouraged the employment of half a million community health workers. Eight more Institutes of

Technology were given the 'go-ahead'. Programmes to introduce school mid-day meals were extended. A massive rural employment guarantee programme was introduced.

Aid to Learning

1. How was the first Manmohan Singh Government different from the Bharatiya Janata Party Rule?
2. Trace the changing face of democracy in India under the different governments.

Exercise

1. Explain briefly why India is a democracy.
2. Name three factors which can point to a change in politics in 1989.
3. Consider the advantages and disadvantages of the reservation system.
4. Explain with examples the impact of political violence and terrorism on Indian Governments from 1989.
5. (a) Explain with examples the main problems faced by the Janata Dal-led Government of 1989.

   (b) Explain why this government collapsed so quickly.
6. Explain with examples the main problems faced by the BJP-led Government of 1998–2004. Which one of these was the most serious? Justify your choice with a reason supported by evidence.
7. Read these two viewpoints.

   View-point 1: Of the three main administrations between 1990 and 2004, the Government led by the BJP was the most successful.

   View-point 2: Of the three main administrations between 1990 and 2004, the Government led by the BJP was the least successful.

   Which view-point do you most agree with? Give reasons for your answer.

   (Make your judgement using specific examples to support your arguments.)

Chapter 2 — Threats to Indian Democracy

Key Question

To what extent is nationalism in India incompatible with the Indian Constitution's commitment to secularism?

Nationalism in India has, in present times, taken on a strong religious colour. It has become more of a majority pro-Hindu movement which seems to threaten minority religious communities, especially Muslims and Christians. The striving for an exclusive Hindu 'nation' has given rise to anti-Muslim and anti-Christian riots and acts of violence on many occasions. Some certainly do want to turn the secular republic of India into a Hindu state that would challenge the Constitution as well as the plural party system in India.

Aid to Learning

1. What do Indian politicians who want India to be secular believe in?
2. Who have been the key players in the Indian 'nationalist' movement?
3. Can 'nationalism' benefit India in the future?

Nationalism

Nationalism can be considered as an ideology highlighting above all an individual's loyalty and devotion to the nation-state, and retaining the important characteristics that make that nation strong and different. Nationalistic sentiments in India go deep into its ancient history as the birthplace of the Indus Valley and Vedic Civilisations and four major world religions: Hinduism, Buddhism, Jainism and Sikhism. In the long struggle for freedom against the British, nationalism united the people of India. Further, Gandhi's strict adherence to democracy, religious and ethnic equality and brotherhood as well as his rejection of caste-based discrimination offered a way to convert that unity into the new independent India.

National leaders such as Sardar Vallabhbhai Patel and Jawaharlal Nehru brought together generations of Indians from across the regions, provided a strong leadership base and gave the country political direction.

The freedom that came on 15 August, 1947 could have been a triumph of the Indian nationalistic sentiments but it also included the Partition. The eventual separation of India into India and Pakistan was the final outcome of a long-standing policy of the British to 'divide and rule'. Seeds of communal discord and disharmony had been planted. Gandhi was soon assassinated by a Hindu nationalist for this supposed sympathy for the Muslims.

Hindu Nationalism

The notion of Hindutva gained prominence in the 1990s. Hindutva seeks to define Indian culture and values in essentially Hindu terms. This championing of Hindutva lies at the heart of the BJP philosophy. Two events, listed below, brought the BJP and the ideology of Hindutva to international attention. The third incident, when the BJP was in power, exposed the level of sympathy and support it extended towards the Hindus in inter-religious strife.

1. In 1992, the Babri Masjid in Ayodhya was destroyed when a political rally became violent, despite a commitment to the Supreme Court that the mosque would not be harmed. In the ensuing communal riots in many cities, including Mumbai and Delhi, more than 2000 people were killed. Since then, the issue has not gone away with on-going debates as to who was responsible and on-going disputes about the site.
2. In 2002, communal violence erupted in Gujarat, triggered by an attack on Hindu pilgrims aboard a train. Inter-communal violence broke out rapidly, with hundreds killed, tens of thousands fleeing their homes and much property damaged or destroyed.

    Inter-communal violence continues in India to this day. A recent twist to this horror is an increase in violence against Christians.

Secularism

The 42nd amendment to the Preamble to the Indian Constitution in 1976 declared that India was to be a secular country, prohibiting discrimination against members of a particular religion, race, caste, sex or place of birth and granting every adult citizen (18 years or more) the right to vote. Secularism was to encourage Indian society to accept equality amongst all religions and to practise religious tolerance. It was intended that secular politics would prevent religious philosophies or bodies from influencing governmental policies. Secularism would keep India united and successful.

Gandhi and Nehru preferred to keep India secular without a state religion, though Indian citizens were free to follow any religion of their birth or adoption. Hence, India remained politically secular but in their personal lives its people continued to be deeply religious.

Over the years, the policies of the various party leaders have inflamed the communal and caste-related passions of the people. Often, these passions are encouraged to gain votes. Such 'politicisation' of the religious and the caste-based issues has challenged India's secular and democratic values and threatened the nation's stability as Nehru feared they would. Due to caste, the communalist and fundamentalist parts of India are far from united, with caste conflicts and communal violence becoming intense.

Key Question

How far have insurgency and terrorist activities weakened the stability of the Indian Republic?

In addition to caste and communal conflicts, parts of India have been or are still being troubled by political violence as groups campaign for independence from Delhi. Andhra Pradesh, Maharashtra, Orissa (now Odisha), Chhattisgarh, Jharkhand and Bihar have all been exposed to insurgency at the hands of the communist Naxalite groups. Islamic fundamentalist groups have provoked violence for the cause of Kashmir independence. In India's troubled Northeast, the United Liberation Front of Assam (ULFA) have fought for the secession of Assam, and the National Socialist Council of Nagalim (Isak-Muivah) demands Naga independence.

In addition, bomb attacks against the army and the railways and the 2008 and 2011 Mumbai terrorist attacks, have all hurt India. Nevertheless, India still has a democratically elected central government to govern the country and the last three elected central governments have completed their full five years' term. Despite its wounds, has the Indian Republic shown that it can and will survive?

Aid to Learning

1. What do you understand by:
   (a) Insurrection
   (b) Terrorism
   (c) Stable Indian Republic
2. Why have some groups been willing to use violence and create terror to achieve their aims?
3. How far have Indian governments dealt with problems of caste discrimination?
4. Why have Indian governments resisted the demands for independence in parts of the country?
5. How far have Indian governments addressed the underlying issues behind the Naxalite threat?

Words of Advice

The following study on caste conflicts and wars cites examples of violence and extremism. The information thus provided as well as your own research can form a basis to answer the questions given earlier.

Caste Conflicts and Wars

The Caste Issue

Castes have become a major force in Indian politics with political parties seeking and depending increasingly on their votes. The members of different caste-groups have, for their part, demanded to be a part of the political system. The political parties ignore them only at their own peril. For many political parties, power has been achieved through 'vote bank politics', with electoral strategy aimed deliberately at attracting the votes of various castes.

The drawback of this has been that caste divisions and communal conflicts have intensified. Political parties have openly offered themselves as the 'political voice' of various castes and have manipulated situations in the corresponding regions to gain power in the State Legislatures. The challenge for the responsible leaders has been to find answers that will keep these caste parties happy, reduce caste discrimination and still win enough votes.

Examples of Cross-Political Party Alliances built around Caste Problems

In Uttar Pradesh, as explained earlier, Mayawati tried hard to ease the misery of the Dalits. She held the view that the Dalits were best served by close association with the upper castes, the Brahmins. Mayawati claimed that the Yadavs were the main tormentors of the Dalits as they were the owners of most of the land in the region. Mayawati championed a quota system based on economic factors. It was argued that the underprivileged could then benefit regardless of caste or creed. The recommendation was supported by Congress and the BJP. A 'Reservation Policy' was issued in October 2008. If private companies wanted to establish new industrial or business units, then in return for grants or benefits, they had to reserve 30 per cent of the posts to be equally divided among OBCs, SCs and the minority community. The aim was to reduce the number of the unemployed in the region.

In Northern India, Janata Dal-United (JD-U) in Bihar along with its alliance partner the Samata Party (October 30, 2003), and as a constituent of the National Democratic Alliance, defeated the RJD-led government in November, 2005, aided by its partner, the BJP. The JD-U mainly enjoyed the support of the Kurmis (a backward caste) while at the same time benefitted from the support extended by the Bhumihars (an upper caste) and the Rajputs towards the BJP. The JD-U took over from the Rashtriya Janata Dal (RJD) which was supported by the Yadav caste, one of the most influential of the OBCs.

In southern India, the Dravida Munnetra Kazagham (DMK), a state political party of Tamil Nadu and Pondicherry (now Puducherry), is a Dravidian party founded as a breakaway faction from the Dravidar Kazhagam. In the 2004 parliamentary elections, DMK formed an alliance with Congress and others, winning all 40 seats including Pondicherry. In 2006, the same alliance won in the state assembly elections and the DMK for the first time formed a minority government in the state with help from Congress. The DMK-Congress alliance was also successful in the 2009 parliamentary elections, securing a majority of the Lok Sabha seats. However, in the Tamil Nadu legislative assembly election in 2011, the party lost power again.

Caste Problems and Politics: Points to Think About

The following points in relation to the symbiotic relationship between the caste parties and the major political parties need to be considered.

1. The vast numbers of caste voters are too great for the Indian politicians to ignore. Do blocks of caste-based votes corrupt Indian politics?
2. The OBCs have become better off as a result of the reservation system, even though they are heavily disadvantaged in terms of education. The top sections of this group have done well in economic terms. Has positive discrimination helped India to reduce the social and economic inequalities caused by caste-based discrimination?
3. In Uttar Pradesh, close ties between the Dalits and the Brahmins brought Mayawati into power. How do such alliances help make reforms possible?
4. Even though the Indian Government passed an 'Atrocities against Dalit Law' in 1990, its implementation has been far from effective with a very poor conviction rate. Why is it so and what does it tell us about contemporary India?
5. 'Having taken a principled stand in foreign policy against racial discrimination and apartheid, India should not hide behind a false sense of Third World sovereignty in discussing the real problems of how to end caste discrimination effectively in a complex society.' (Manmohan Singh, 2006). What was Singh saying about (a) Caste, (b) India?

An Example of 'Caste War'

India's entrenched caste system has endured countless conflicts, sufferings and atrocities. Even though government reservation policies have improved the lives of the backward castes, caste-based hatred and intolerance still cause outright violence, bordering on war.

Bihar: Yadavs, Dalits and Naxalites

Many communities in Bihar and Madhya Pradesh have lived in fear, suffering violence and atrocities from time to time. Lalu Yadav, a major political figure of the region, openly raised his voice against these vicious wrongs.

Yadav was born into a backward caste family which made its living from tending livestock. He became the Chief Minister of Bihar in 1990 and remained in office till 1997. He has been a Lok Sabha MP and was the Minister of Railways from 2004 to 2009. For over a decade, he had warned of continuing violence if the Yadav caste landowners failed to give adequate rights to their landless, Dalit, manual workers. Lalu Yadav

Fig. 1.6   Lalu Prasad Yadav

championed the cause of the poorest caste, enlisted their support in gaining political power and consequently berated the upper and the middle castes for creating a situation which he compared to the erstwhile evil system of Apartheid in South Africa.

Organised Dalit resistance materialised itself into secret camps in Madhya Pradesh where Dalit women (considered to be the most vulnerable members of the backward castes) were trained to use fire-arms and taught self-respect. The driving force in some areas had been training given by the Naxalite rebels.

Several Naxalite leaders persuaded field workers to withdraw their labour and protest against their living and working conditions. Many landowners had started to be on the defensive with their estate headquarters stockpiled with arms to head off attacks, if any. But they went much further, organising violent action against their own workers. They felt justified in this because the manual labourers were challenging the landowners' authority and status in the community. Violence further escalated in Bihar when landowner 'death squads', known as 'Ranvir Sena', emerged.

They were recognised as 'terrorist' organisations and banned by the Bihar State Government in 1995. The Ranvir Sena rampaged through Dalit villages, murdering and injuring the inhabitants indiscriminately. One of the worst incidents was recorded in December 1997, when Ranvir Sena men attacked Laxmanpur-Bathe village, leaving 61 dead, including 16 children and 33 women, 8 of whom were pregnant.

Terrorism and Insurgence

Terrorism is defined as the 'peace time equivalent of war crime.' If you accept this definition, India has suffered many 'war crimes' over the last decades. Bombings, explosions, shootings and organised attacks have left death and devastation in their wake.

By 2006, it was calculated that over 230 of India's 608 districts had been affected by terrorist or insurgent activities.

Between 1997 and 2007, over 630 people were killed by major terror attacks. There were seven massive bomb attacks on trains. Some of these trains were travelling from cities such as Mumbai, Godhra and Kurnool. In 2007, there was a bomb attack on the Samjhauta Express, a train that runs twice a week connecting Delhi and Lahore. Overall, the loss of civilian lives since Independence has been estimated to be more than 80 000.

Sometimes involving suicide bombers, terrorists have attacked religious communities and shrines, economic targets such as coal mines and nuclear power stations, army depots and camps, hotels, tourist attractions and airports.

Examples of Terrorist Groups

Punjab

The terrorist-secessionist movement in the Punjab, fighting for Khalistan as a separate Sikh nation, was a long drawn out one until its defeat in 1993. Khalistan terrorist groups, such as the Babbar Khalsa International (BKI), are still active, probably with outside support. In December 2011, Delhi police arrested two operatives of the BKI suspecting that the Punjab-based terror outfit was planning to assassinate some political and religious leaders in Delhi and Punjab.

Kashmir

From early to mid-2000, it was reported that a home-grown Islamic terrorist group, Indian Mujahideen (IM), had been involved with the Hizbul Mujahideen in Kashmir. The organisation's aim is to carry out terrorist actions against non-Muslims and to create an Islamic caliphate across South Asia.

IM is responsible for dozens of bomb attacks throughout India since 2005 and has caused the deaths of hundreds of innocent civilians. In September 2011, the United States placed the IM on its organised terrorist list. The IM claimed responsibility for the July 2008 Bangalore, Ahmedabad and Delhi (September 2008) serial blasts, the 2010 Jama Masjid attack and the 2011 Mumbai serial blasts, amongst others.

In 2005, the Lashkar-e-Toiba, a Kashmiri militant group, had separated into two splinter groups (Al Mansurin and Al Nasirin) involved in terrorism to free Kashmir from Indian rule. Many other smaller militant groups, some based in Pakistan, were active in various attacks. All of these terrorists were allied in some way to the United Jihad Council (UJC). The Indian Government blamed the Lashkar-e-Toiba (LeT) and Jaish-e-Mohammad for the December 2001 attack on the Indian Parliament in New Delhi.

Maoists (Naxalites)

Maoist terrorist groups, also named Naxalites, have remained a major threat to the stability of India. In 2006, India's intelligence agency estimated that 20 000 armed cadre Naxalites were operating in addition to 50 000 regular cadres. Their growing influence prompted Indian Prime Minister Manmohan Singh to declare them to be the most serious internal threat to India's national security. In 2009, Naxalites were active across approximately 180 districts in ten states of India. By July 2011, however, the number of Naxal affected areas was reduced to 83 districts across nine states. However, the Maoists virtually came to have full control over the state of Jharkhand.

Fig. 1.7   Naxal cadre under training

The Naxals transformed 16 out of the 22 districts of Jharkhand into a 'guerrilla zone'. Naxal violence in Jharkhand has claimed the lives of nearly 700 people, which includes over 200 policemen. They attack police stations, blow up government buildings, railway stations and hijack passenger trains. They have used civilians as hostages and human shields while demanding protection payments.

Local police forces have been incapable of countering these terrorist activities, despite the creation in 2005 of the Salwa Judum militia organisation, armed and trained by the State Government of Jharkhand to counter Naxalite violence. The Naxalite groups continue to control vast areas of rural land. These are usually the poorest regions of the nation where many tribes have been living in abject poverty.

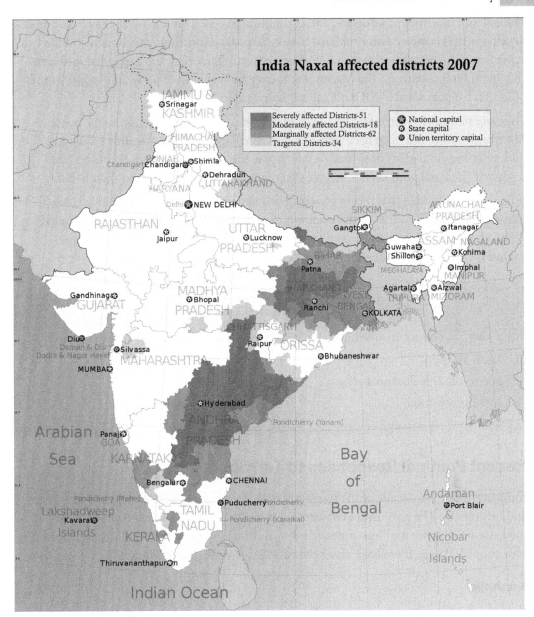

Map 1.1   Map showing the districts where the Naxalite Movement is active (2007)

Terrorism and Economic Development

India's governments have promoted massive industrialisation and endorsed extensive investment by private entrepreneurs. New global enterprises are encouraged to invest in India. Projects are encouraged by relaxed regulations and incentives and developments are sponsored by profit-seeking multi-national companies.

The Indian Government wants to protect the rural poor within the umbrella of economic development. However, two problems have emerged, the one being terrorism and the other being the opposition to new 'outsider' projects. Terrorism has expanded into areas rich in mineral resources. The Maoist insurgency has capitalised on what they see as theft of local resources, local tribal land and capitalist exploitation.

To create new mines, farmland was seized with very little compensation to the owners. Mine profits have not been used to develop local villages and their facilities. Villagers in developing rural areas now tend to look upon any new project with suspicion and mistrust. The rural poor do not believe that new enterprises could be to their benefit.

It has been contended that recent governments have been hesitant to take on a 'zero tolerance' approach, scared of the backlash of opposition from its minority 'vote bank'. Political parties have not really come together to create a framework for joint action against terrorism. Terrorist attacks have hence continued at regular intervals.

Activities

From Map 1.1, choose an area highly affected by Naxal Terrorism. Investigate the effects on:

1. Local People
2. Economic Development
3. Law Enforcement

Recent Political Responses to Terrorism

India in the second decade of the twenty-first century is still in the clutches of terrorism and insurgency. The government has not underestimated the political damage caused by the extreme violence and fear engendered by indiscriminate terror. While there have been some hopeful signs, there have also been further terrorist developments.

Kashmir

In Kashmir, the acts of violence have become relatively fewer. In this, the improved relations between India and Pakistan have been of help. The agreed ceasefire has been a much needed step-forward and provided a scope for negotiation. International pressure had been put on the Pakistan Government to end military support and act against militant training camps, particularly in its northern territory. The Indian Government feels that the Kashmir insurgency would not cease whilst Pakistan tries to play a 'proxy' conflict and support terrorist activity against India behind the scenes. Recent political changes in Pakistan have added to improved relations between Pakistan and India.

International Support

The Indian Government has realised that it needs external expertise to counter highly sophisticated terrorism. Israel has provided military anti-terrorism surveillance equipment to the Indian Army.
Indian forces have also benefited from their involvement in US-run exercises. Selected troops have been trained by specialised US personnel in anti-terrorist combat strategies.

A new government strategy to counter Islamic terrorism came in September 2008 with a new counter-terrorism centre in New Delhi acting as a single reference point for anti-terrorist strategies.

Exercise

1. Explain in a sentence each of the terms given below.
   (a) Nationalism
   (b) Secularism
   (c) Insurrection
   (d) Terrorism
2. Explain the following in a paragraph each.
   (a) Why has the destruction of the 'Babri Masjid' caused such problems?
   (b) What is the meaning behind this statement: 'the BJP is a 'pro-Hindu' party?'
3. 'India has too many political parties for democratic governments to be very successful.' How far do you agree with this view? Give reasons for your answer.
4. 'Religion-based nationalism' will not help India in the twenty-first century.' Consider this claim.
5. Read the following statements:
   Statement 1: Terrorism will only be defeated in India by the use of force.
   Statement 2: Terrorism will only be defeated in India by major social and economic reforms.
   Which statement do you agree with the most? Give reasons for your answer. (You should try to make a judgement using examples to support your arguments.)
6. 'Caste problems are the most important issues facing Indian Governments.' How far do you agree with this statement? Give reasons for your answer.

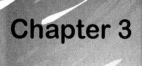

Chapter 3 Political Participation

Key Question

Can Indian democracy be sustained in the face of so much of political violence?

The May 2009 general elections gave India another democratically elected government with a wide range of representatives voted for by approximately 60 per cent of the Indian population. Such a result is strong evidence of sustained democracy. Unfortunately, despite the huge deployment of Indian army troops on electoral duties, the elections also saw political violence, riots and deaths.

This chapter concentrates on the 2009-Indian general elections, identifying the big personalities involved and the main issues the parties fought over.

Aid to Learning

- Identify what the main manifesto promises of each main political 'alliance' were.
- Why was there violence and intimidation during the 2009 elections? Do you agree that such incidents might be seen as bringing India's democratic election procedures into disrepute? Give reasons for your answer.
- 'Participation in the 2009 Indian elections was not the same over all the regions of India.' Why was this?

Words of Advice

The questions above require evidence and examples to show a good understanding of the topic.

Electoral Malpractice

Elections in India are meant to be free and fair, as laid down in the Constitution. Electronic ID cards were introduced to reduce fraud caused by impersonation of voters. Electronic Voting Machines were likewise introduced to make the voting process simpler and less time-consuming. Election officers were removed if they were found to be biased in favour of any particular political party. Electoral rolls were scrutinised more thoroughly.

Fig. 1.8   Women showing their voter cards

However, in spite of all these measures, electoral malpractices did occur during the 2009 elections.

Main Types of Electoral Malpractice

- Booth capturing
- Vote rigging
- Bribes
- 'Bogus' voters
- Systematic attacks on minorities
- Families not registering female votes
- Taking too long to count votes
- Attacks on candidates
- Street violence against a particular minority
- Corrupt election officers.

Aid to Learning

Look at the different forms of electoral malpractice listed above. Identify at least six malpractices that occurred during the 2009 Indian general elections. Complete the spider diagram given here, showing each point at the end of each 'arm'.

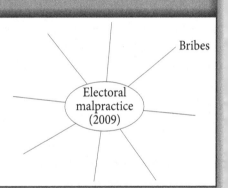

The General Elections of May 2009

Electoral Participation

714 million Indians were eligible to vote in 828 804 polling centres with six million officials and army personnel taking part. Candidates were selected from a wide range of political parties. Photo-electoral rolls were put in place. Five polling days were set aside, three in April and two in May, 2009.

Ballot papers were printed with the names of the candidates and the corresponding symbols of their parties. The voters had to press the electronic button against the name

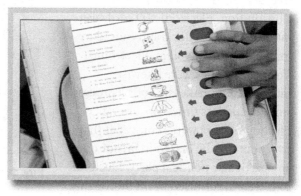

Fig. 1.9   Poll officials inspect an Electronic Voting Machine (EVM)

and the symbol of the candidate of their choice. Then, they were given an ink mark on the index finger so that they could not vote again. The average election turnout over all the five phases was around 59.7 per cent. There was a fairly high rural turnout. The results of the election were announced within three days following the last polling day.

Political Campaigning

The May 2009 elections witnessed three major political party campaigns at a time that was crucial for India with its massively expanding economy that felt the strain of the global financial crisis. Moreover, India's relations with Pakistan were at a new low since the Mumbai attacks in November 2008.

Domestic security concerns were highlighted soon after polling opened when Maoist rebels launched attacks in many of the eastern states. At least 16 people, including nine paramilitary troopers and five polling officials, were killed in eastern India in a wave of election day attacks. In Jharkhand, a hotbed of Maoist activity, the rebels ambushed a bus carrying security forces for duty at polling stations, killing seven soldiers and two civilians. In Bihar, two security personnel were shot dead and another wounded by the rebels in Gaya district. Maoists declared that they were defending the rights of the neglected tribal people and the landless farmers.

Review of the 'Big' Three Campaigns

The **United Progressive Alliance** (UPA) campaign defended its record in the government by highlighting economic growth, containment of terrorism and maintenance of security. The UPA commended its massive $2.2 billion rural employment guarantee programme.

It campaigned on the basis that it was the most competent alliance to see India through its current problems. It argued that the electorate could have confidence in the 'Gandhi/ Singh' partnership. The opposition coalition, the **National Democratic Alliance** (NDA), greatly criticised India's internal security against terrorism, complaining that the UPA had been totally ineffective with regard to the 2008 Mumbai terrorist attacks. The NDA also highlighted what they saw as the inefficiency of the government in carrying out economic reforms. The NDA accused the Prime Minister of being far too influenced by Sonia Gandhi, the leader of the Congress Party.

Fig. 1.10   Sonia Gandhi (right) with her son Rahul canvassing for the Congress Party

Fig. 1.11   The BJP, led by L.K Advani (centre)

BJP also accused the Congress of using Muslims as 'vote banks'. It claimed that, as a party, the BJP was against 'vote banks', quite regardless of their own use of the Hindu 'vote bank'.

The **Third Front** hoped to create a non-BJP, non-Congress government by attracting many

local and regional parties. It brought together demands from the left-wing and the regional parties. It consisted of CPI(M), CPI, JD (Secular), TDP, BSP and other religional parties. Their efforts centred upon attracting a wider range of support for regional and minority issues. The 'Third Front' challenge depended on gaining enough votes to have a chance of forming a government if the UPA or the NDA did not win enough seats. But, the 'vote-splitting' by the Third Front backfired. In Maharashtra, for

Fig. 1.12   Mayawati, the leader of India's circa 160 million Dalits

example, the BSP allowed the Congress to make gains in many of its seats without getting a majority.

Yet, the Third Front campaign, like that of many regional parties, took note of the grass-root grievances, such as those demanded by Chotte Lal Singh Patel, a village elder from the outskirts of Varanasi. He had spoken for many ordinary village people demanding basic amenities such as electricity, clean water, and opportunities such as employment for young people. Many Dalit groups voted against the Congress. They were more in favour of the secular parties, including that of the Dalit politician Mayawati.

Examples of Campaign Slogans

1. The Congress Party bought the rights for the sound track 'Jai Ho'('Let Their Be Victory') from the movie Slumdog Millionaire. It was used as the official campaign tune by the party. The Congress hoped that the popular song would galvanise the masses during the almost one month-long election season.
2. To counter the Congress' selection, the BJP used the phrase 'Kushal Neta, Nirnayak Sarkaar' ('Able Leader, Decisive Government'). The BJP intended to use L. K. Advani's name and image as the main focus.

The Election Result: The Winner

1. After all the votes were counted, the Congress Party returned to power in a Coalition Government with almost an overall majority of seats.

Table 1.3   2009 Lok Sabha elections results

Party	Seats	Seat change
United Progressive Alliance	262	+ 80
National Democratic Alliance	159	−17
The 'Third Front'	79	−30
Fourth Front (SP, RJD, LJP)	27	−37
Other Parties and Independent Seats	16	+9

2. The Indian National Congress dominated the government based on its strong showing. The UPA was able to put together a comfortable majority with support from 322 out of 543 members of the House. The new government looked more stable than the previous one.
3. Manmohan Singh was sworn in as the Prime Minister. He became the first Prime Minister since Nehru in 1962 to be re-elected after completing a full five-year term.

Examples of Election Violence

As the 2009 elections approached, Hindu extremists continued to mobilise anti-Christian support. Back in September 2008, a crisis had occurred in **Orissa** where extremist Hindu groups carried out anti-Christian violence.

For example, in Kandhamal, anti-Christian massacres claimed more than 100 lives. More than 18 000 were injured and 50 000 displaced. Another report said that around 11 000 people were still living in relief camps, as of October 2008.

In **Karnataka**, at least 28 attacks were recorded in August and September 2008, according to a report by People's Union of Civil Liberties.

In early May 2009, the government banned the CPI (Maoist) organisation after weeks of violence, death and constant disruption of the elections in many rural districts. The impact of political violence during the 2009 elections can be illustrated through the example of Aliya Bibi. Both she and her daughter were among the dozens shot and beaten in what was an attempt by supporters of **West Bengal's** ruling Communist Party of India-Marxist (CPM) to stop opponents from casting their votes. The attacks were centred on Satengabari and its neighbouring villages in the Nandigram district.

This is where the communists and their opponents of the Trinamul Congress (TMC) clashed over plans by the West Bengal Government to evict local farmers to make way for a chemical company. There were similar clashes throughout the state over its government's attempts to force through development plans against villagers' wishes.

Conclusion

Democracy had been sustained, but all the problems faced in 1989 had not been resolved. The positive changes and reforms that the governments attempted have often been very slow in being carried out. Huge strides in liberalising the economy have created vast growth and encouraged considerable foreign direct investment. But investment in human resources has not been enough and more reforms are required to reduce the vast poverty and human misery experienced by hundreds of millions of Indian citizens.

> India needs to launch a second generation of reforms after undertaking an in-depth analysis of what has gone wrong until now during the course of the on-going round of reforms. These reforms can help India grow at the rate of 10 per cent per annum over next two decades or so. This would make India's economy by the year 2020 the world's largest, after the US and China.
>
> *Subramaniam Swamy*
> *Former Union Minister for Commerce*

The report to the people 2009–2010 (at the end of the first year of the UPA's second term) gave an indication that reforms could make a difference. The report outlined a vast range of projects and reforms particularly across social, cultural and economic sectors of India, for example, Right of Children to Free and Compulsory Education (RTE) Act, 2009, whereby 7 400 new primary schools and 11 847 upper primary schools were opened.

However, the second term of the UPA administration has not always gone to plan. The UPA has faced opposition on several counts, rising prices being one. Thirteen opposition parties called for a nationwide strike on 27 April, 2010, to protest the Congress-led United Progressive Alliance (UPA) Government's 'failure' to control rising prices. The 13 parties accounted for a combined 87 seats in the 545-member Lok Sabha. The BJP, which had 116 seats, has announced support for any move against the government on the issue of rising prices. The Government also faces a steady erosion of business confidence abroad as it has failed to push through much needed economic reforms and infrastructure investment.

In addition, outbreaks of caste violence have repeatedly been reported, especially in rural areas, such as in Saniyanna village, Hisar, where a Dalit youth was attacked with a sharp-edged weapon. His arm was nearly chopped off for drinking water from an earthen pot belonging to an upper caste family.

Indian governance has a long way to go to make India a country which protects and benefits all of her people, but democracy has been sustained. If the views of the former President of India, Dr APJ Abdul Kalam, are to become a reality, a great deal more will be required of central and state legislatures.

> A developed India by 2020, or even earlier, is not a dream. It need not even be mere vision in the minds of many Indians. It is a mission we can all take up and succeed.
>
> *Dr APJ Abdul Kalam*
> *Indian President 2002–2007*

That mission has to address fundamental issues, such as the financial gulf between India's different social classes, with immense poverty at odds with the accumulation of great wealth by the educated and professional elite. India has entered the twenty-first century as a major player on the world's stage. And it is to India's interpretation of democracy and adaptability to cope with the global economic opportunities that have mainly provided the platform for moving forward.

Unit 2 · Economic Development

Aims of the Unit

- Understand and differentiate between the concepts of economic growth and economic development
- Describe the changing nature of Indian economy and the role of economic planning in development
- Evaluate the economic reform measures and identify their shortcomings
- Explain the strategies followed in different phases of development in India and reason out the shift in the emphasis
- Analyse and assess the performance of the Indian economy post-reforms
- Recognise the importance of sustaining development and identify emerging issues

Key Concepts

Gross Domestic Product: The total value of output produced by all domestic firms in a country in one year

Gross National Product: The sum of GDP and net property income from abroad

Balance of payments: A record of all inflows and outflows in a country arising from economic activity in the domestic and foreign sectors during one year

Per capita income: Result obtained by dividing the GDP of a country by the population of that country

Foreign exchange reserves: The amount of foreign currencies and, traditionally, gold that the central bank of that country holds

Rate of economic growth: The increase in GDP/GNP from one time period to another

Economic growth: A quantitative concept indicating increases in real output of goods and services (GDP per capita) over a time period

Economic development: A qualitative concept, contrary to economic growth, indicating progressive changes in the socio-economic structure of a country

Public sector: Inclusive of all those economic activities, where the ownership of means of production combined with its management lies completely with the government

Private sector: Driven by profit-motive and characterised by private ownership of the means of production

Economic planning: The conscious and deliberate choice of economic priorities by some public authorities (Barbara Wootten)

Nationalisation: The act of taking assets or an industry into the public ownership of a national government

Import substitution: A strategy for economic development encouraging industrial growth within a nation in order to reduce imports of manufactures, save foreign exchange, provide jobs, and reduce dependency

Devaluation of the domestic currency: The fall in the value of domestic currency vis-à-vis the foreign currency, whereby the value of exports rises as domestic goods become cheaper to foreigners and more foreign exchange flows in

Trade deficit: The situation where a country's imports are greater than its exports leading to an outflow of domestic currency to foreign markets

Fiscal deficit: The shortfall in government revenues over its expenditure which when filled up through borrowings in the government's account, crowds out private investment.

Time Line

1947 to 1991 – Era of Economic Planning and the so called 'License Raj'

1991 – Introduction of Economic Reforms: Liberalisation, Privatisation and Globalisation

1991 to 2012 – Post-Reform Era: 'Shining India' with growing challenges of poverty and inequality

2010 – India becomes fourth largest in the world in terms of real GDP with 8.4 per cent growth

Introduction

From an international perspective, India's growth performance of the last two decades ranks amongst the top six in the world, along with China, Korea, Thailand, Singapore and Vietnam. India is now only second to China in growth rates and is expected to exceed China during the first two decades of the twenty-first century.

India's story of development began soon after its Independence in 1947 with a 'big push' given to it by the political leaders and industrialists who advocated economic planning.

In this earlier phase of planned economic development in India, the main emphasis was on economic growth. Reduction in inequalities of income and wealth, elimination of poverty and creation of employment opportunities were also mentioned as objectives of planning but they were never given a high priority. Much of this growth has been due to macroeconomic policy changes since 1991, but also due to favourable international circumstances and the global environment.

There was a crisis in the year 1990–1991 which manifested itself in various forms such as problems pertaining to severe balance of payments, declining industrial production, rising inflationary pressures and the sharp deceleration in real GDP, falling as low as 0.5 per cent in 1991–1992. The new development strategy that was adopted was an Export-led Growth Strategy leading India towards globalisation. This followed a scheme of comprehensive liberalisation measures to improve the economic health of the country.

Table 2.1   External Trade with other countries during 2007–08 and 2008–09

Region	Exports (April–Feb)		Imports (April–Feb)	
	2007–08	*2008–09(P)*	*2007–08(P)*	*2008–09(P)*
1. Europe	1 33 151	1 65 925	1 75 335	2 23 813
2. Africa	38 062	44 922	51 519	60 151
3. America	98 900	1 14 966	79 780	1 21 381
4. Asia and Asean	2 96 287	3 57 982	5 43 551	7 39 622
5. CIS & Baltics	6 101	7 623	14 238	28 793
6. Other	1 482	4 346	2 666	4 710
Total	5 77 889	6 96 498	8 70 399	11 98 360

Since 1991, the government has undertaken both stabilisation and structural reforms as two components of the economic reform package. The initial period of five years after the reforms saw a remarkable acceleration of GDP growth and all the major sectors (agriculture, industry, services) grew at a noticeably faster pace. In contrast, the average growth performance in the period 1996–2000 was disappointing, characterised by a fall in agricultural growth to 1.4 per cent, a significant fall in industrial growth to 4.9 per cent and buoyancy of services. This growth in services was much faster than in the case of industry, a pattern that raises questions of sustainability, as no economy can continue to grow this way for long. Table 2.1 highlights the growing deficit in terms of imports and exports. Thus, the nation needs to launch a second generation of reforms.

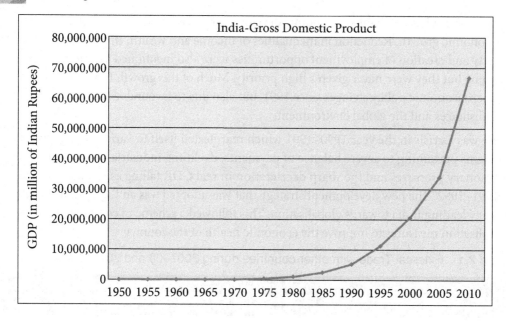

Fig. 2.1   India's GDP

As India faces the new century, the Indian economy stands at crossroads. Either it can live with continued poverty and a low growth trap or take the high road to achieve prosperity, global prominence and a more egalitarian society through accelerated reforms and by energising innovation.

Economic Growth and Development

The term economic development was for long considered identical with economic growth. It is now no longer considered to be a rise in national output. Instead, it includes certain crucial variables which determine the well-being of the people. There are various indicators regarding the economic wealth of a nation, the prosperity of its people and its standing in the international forum. Most common of these are the Gross National Product (GNP), Gross Domestic Product (GDP), the balance of payments, foreign exchange reserves, rate of economic growth, per capita income, etc.

Economic growth refers to increases in the quantity of output (goods and services) produced over a period of time (usually a year) and is usually expressed as a percentage change in real GDP. Growth is calculated in real terms, i.e. inflation-adjusted terms, in order to net out the effect of inflation on the price of the goods and services produced. It has the potential to alleviate poverty, increase employment opportunities and labour productivity.

Economic development is a complex process. It originally referred to the process by which an economy would shift from a primarily agricultural output to one with a large proportion of secondary goods, i.e. a process of industrialisation. In this context, growth was used as a narrow definition of development.

Aid to Learning

Read the information given below and answer the questions that follow.

Fig. 2.2   India's GDP contributors

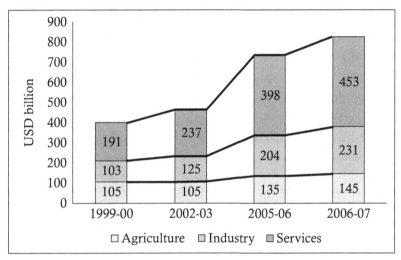

GDP Contributors (2003–07)
- Industry: 26% ($138B) growth at 16.2%
- Service: 55% (269B) growing at 16.3%
- Agriculture: 19% (73B) growing at 10.2%

Huge Services contribution is a characteristic of a developed economy

Smoke is emitted by a power plant smokestack against the backdrop of monsoon rain clouds in Kolkata. The smoke adds to the so-called Asian Brown Cloud, a layer of air pollution covering parts of the northern Indian Ocean, India, Pakistan, and parts of South Asia, Southeast Asia, and China. The chief of the UN panel on climate change said the cloud was a matter of concern but it would take up to about five years to know if its impact on climate change was serious or negligible.

A man prepares to cast a fishing net into the polluted water of river Yamuna with the historic Taj Mahal in the background. The Yamuna is a major tributary of the Ganges and is polluted by sewage water from the Indian capital, Delhi.

According to a World Bank study, estimated costs of water pollution in India were as high as eight billion dollars in 1995. Both population and economy have grown tremendously since then, putting increasing stress on India's major rivers.

1. What happened to GDP contributors of India between 1999 and 2007?
2. What factors do you think would be responsible for this transformation?
3. From the two images, in what ways did this progress lead to some negative effects on the well-being of the nation?

Many developing countries have failed to increase the 'trickle-down effect' of their increasing incomes. The concept of economic development was, therefore, broadened to portray not only economic growth, but also a reduction in poverty, inequality of income and unemployment.

Development of an economy is influenced by both economic and non-economic factors. Among the economic factors, the most prominent ones are the available capital stock and the rate of its accumulation, capital-output ratio in various sectors, conditions in foreign trade and economic system. In addition, some non-economic factors such as size and quality of human resources, political freedom, social organisation, technical know-how, general education, absence of corruption and above all, the very will to develop play an important role in determining the pace and direction of development.

Gross Domestic Product

The Gross Domestic Product (GDP) in a country like India has grown at a faster rate in recent years. With regard to the composition of GDP, the percentage shares of various sectors have changed significantly. The percentage share of agriculture in the total GDP has declined. On the contrary, the percentage share of services in the GDP is rising fast. India's diverse economy encompasses traditional village farming, modern agriculture, handicrafts, a wide range of modern industries, and a multitude of services.

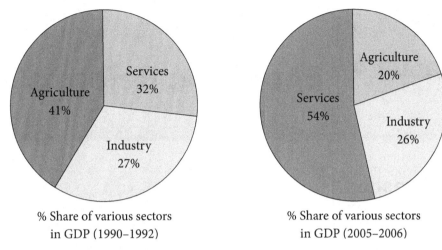

% Share of various sectors
in GDP (1990–1992)

% Share of various sectors
in GDP (2005–2006)

Fig. 2.3   Percentage share of various sectors in GDP

Aid to Learning

1. Define economic growth. How does it differ from economic development?
2. The above pie charts represent a change in the sectoral composition of GDP in India for the years 1990–1991 and 2005–2006. What does this indicate, growth or development?
3. Is a falling share of agriculture a good indicator of the living standards of the people? Explain your answer.
4. List all the other information you think is necessary for you to be able to comment on the well-being of the people of India.

Chapter 4

Economic Reforms

Key Question

What is economic liberalisation and what has been liberalised in India? How has the role of the Indian Government transformed with these economic reforms?

In the 1980s, the Indian economy went through a process of transition from a highly regulated economy in which a number of sanctions had to be acquired before starting a unit of production in any industry. This led to widespread corruption in which the principal beneficiary was the bureaucracy engaged in the grant of concessions.

To unshackle the industrial sector from unnecessary bureaucratic controls, it was imperative for the government to introduce liberalisation to integrate with the world economy and remove the restrictions on Foreign Direct Investment (FDI). The economic reforms comprised three fundamental policy changes namely liberalisation, privatisation and globalisation. In short, this is known as the LPG model of Indian economic development. Several major changes at the domestic level were introduced.

Liberalisation Policy

Liberalisation refers to the relaxation of previous government restrictions, usually in areas of social or economic policy. The term liberalisation has been treated in India in a very broad sense to include the following two variants.

- **Domestic liberalisation:** Reduction of unnecessary controls on pricing, distribution, production and investment while simultaneously increasing the freedom to compete and the pressure of competition. Other domestic reforms included reduction in corporate and personal income tax and wealth tax rates.
- **External liberalisation:** A reduction in controls on imports of raw material, intermediate goods and capital goods, increasing both the competitive pressure on domestic producers and their access to the means of competition, thereby integrating the Indian economy with the world economy.

Major initiatives under liberalisation

- All industrial licensing was abolished except for a short list of five industries for security and strategic reasons, social reasons, hazardous chemicals and environmental reasons. This opened gateways of the economy to foreign competition, forcing considerable restructuring of the private sector.
- De-reservation of Small Scale Industries (SSI) sector to allow them to become more competitive.
- Withdrawing MRTP (Monopolistic and Restrictive Trade Practices) restrictions in order to provide more freedom and a liberal environment to big business houses to undertake expansion, mergers and amalgamations. The largest industrial groups in India are the Ambanis (Reliance Group) followed by the Tatas.

Privatisation

Privatisation refers to the process of transferring ownership of business from the public sector (government) to the private sector (business). It involves the enlargement of the scope of private sector in the growth of the economy and narrowing the role of the public sector to provide social and economic infrastructure with assistance from the private sector. The basic aim of the transfer of ownership was to improve productivity and operational efficiency. This released the large amount of public resources locked up in non-strategic PSEs for redeployment in areas that were of social priority, such as basic health, family welfare, primary education and social and essential infrastructure.

Various forms of privatisation in India

- **Total de-nationalisation:** complete transfer of ownership of a public enterprise to private hands
- **Joint venture:** partial move to private ownership
- **Workers' co-operative:** transfer of ownership to workers
- **Disinvestment:** sale of equity and bond capital invested by the government in a public sector undertaking

Globalisation

Globalisation is defined as the growing economic inter-dependence of countries worldwide through increasing volume and variety of cross-border transactions in goods and services, free international capital flows and a more rapid and widespread diffusion of technology.

Focus

Globalisation as an extension of the process of liberalisation plus internationalism

- Trade barriers in the form of custom duties and quantitative restrictions or quotas were reduced so as to permit free flows of goods and services. This helped in increasing the share of foreign trade as a percentage of the GDP and enabled a developing country like India to acquire quality consumer goods, especially consumer durables.
- An environment for the free flow of technology leading to faster diffusion of knowledge was created. This made the attainment of international standards of production and productivity possible.
- Foreign Direct Investment (FDI) was promoted to help raise capital without incurring international debts.
- Free flow of labour or human resources was promoted to enhance employment.

Aid to Learning

1. What are the major constituents of economic reforms in India?
2. How far, and in what ways, are they linked to each other? Explain your thinking on this.

The principal aim of the economic reforms was for India to benefit from globalisation. To do that, India needed two distinct strands of reforms, namely macroeconomic stabilisation and structural reforms. Stabilisation deals with demand management, reduction of volatility and the encouragement welfare-enhancing growth. Structural reforms deal with sectoral adjustments designed to tackle the problems on the supply side of the economy. They also deal with reorganisation of how the financial services industry is managed in order to strengthen it.

Financial Sector Reforms

Until the early 1990s, the role of the financial system in India was primarily restricted to the function of channelling resources from the surplus to the deficit sectors. Financial markets were characterised by control over pricing of financial assets, barriers to entry, high transaction costs and restrictions on the movement of funds and participants between the market segments. This, apart from inhibiting the development of the markets, also affected their efficiency. The main thrust of reforms in the financial sector was on the following.

- The creation of efficient and stable financial institutions and markets
- Reforms of banking as well as non-banking financial institutions
- Particular focus on imparting operational flexibility and functional autonomy in the banking sector with a view to enhancing efficiency, productivity and profitability
- Reforms in financial markets focused on removal of structural bottlenecks, introduction of new players/instruments, free pricing of financial assets, relaxation of quantitative restrictions, and improvement in trading, clearing and settlement.

Though the public sector dominates in banking, private banks are permitted to operate in it. Foreign Direct Investment (FDI) of up to 74 per cent in the private banks is permitted under the automatic route. In addition, foreign banks are allowed to open a specified number of new branches every year. More than 25 foreign banks with full banking licences and approximately 150 foreign bank branches were in operation by 2010. Under the 1997 WTO Financial Services Agreement, India committed to permitting 12 foreign bank branches annually.

Fiscal Consolidation and Stabilisation

Fiscal consolidation and stabilisation were seen as preconditions for successful reforms and were assigned the highest priority, especially during the initial phase of the reform programme. Some reduction in the fiscal deficit was achieved by systemic improvements, such as:

- The abolition of export subsidies in 1991–1992 and the partial restructuring of the fertiliser subsidy
- Budgetary support to loss-making public sector enterprises
- Sharp reductions in capital expenditures and the transfers to the state governments.

Industrial Policy and Foreign Investment

Industrial policy was subjected to a complete overhaul. Several barriers to entry into industries were removed. Industrial licensing was abolished except for a small number of small-scale sectoral units. The parallel, but separate controls over investment and expansion by larger industrial houses through the Monopolies and Restrictive Trade Practices Act were abolished. The Companies Act was streamlined.

The list of industries reserved for the public sector was drastically reduced. There was a radical restructuring of the public policy towards foreign investment. Earlier, India's policy towards foreign investment had been very selective and had been perceived by foreigners as unfriendly.

Equity participation was limited to about 40 per cent, except in selected high technology or export-oriented sectors. With the beginning of reforms, the foreign investment limit was raised to 51 per cent and then still further a little later. Foreign investment is now permitted in a much larger number of sectors. The Foreign Investment Promotion Board has been set up to facilitate FDI in India. India has also entered into bilateral and multilateral investment guarantee schemes.

Liberalisation and Exchange Rate Policies

The period post-1991 is also marked by a substantial liberalisation of the trade policy. These were necessary to make exports competitive in the international market and also as a part of stabilisation and structural adjustment programmes. Moreover, with India joining the World Trade Organization (WTO) in 1995 as a founder member, it is under obligation to strike down all quantitative restrictions on imports and reduce tariffs so as to 'open up' the economy to world trade and the forces of globalisation. Trade policies were substantially liberalised for all except final consumer goods. The complex import-control regime for imports of raw material and intermediate and capital goods was virtually dismantled. Quantitative restrictions on imports and customs duties were lowered.

The exchange rate regime has undergone complete transformation. The highly controlled regime based on a chronically overvalued exchange rate for the rupee has been dismantled. Two substantial devaluations were followed by the establishment of a dual and then a unified exchange rate regime. In 1994, the rupee became convertible on the current account. Setting up of trade houses and the creation of Export Promotion Zones (EPZs) and Special Economic Zones (SEZs) are other important aspects of the trade liberalisation policies.

Service sectors that have been traditionally subjected to heavy government intervention were opened widely to private sector participation including foreign investors. For example, insurance was a state monopoly and in 1999 the Indian Parliament opened the insurance sector to private and foreign participation.

Tax Reform

Tax reform was undertaken subsequent to the report of a government committee and had the following broad characteristics.
- The number of income tax categories was brought down. Stronger incentives for saving were provided by redefining the base of the wealth tax (which earlier included all personal assets).
- Corporate tax rates, which (in 1991) had been 51.75 per cent for a publicly listed company and 57.5 per cent for closely held companies, were unified at 46 per cent. Corporate taxes were further lowered.
- Excise duties on manufactured goods had hitherto been charged at varying rates on different commodities and most of these duties had been specific rather than ad valorem.

There had been an abundance of exemptions and interpretations of the tax laws. Indirect tax procedures were now simplified and most duties were made ad valorem. The number of excise rates was more than halved. A beginning was made with respect to the taxation of services. The longer-term objective of the government is to move to a full-scale VAT.

Aid to Learning

1. Why do you think the low rates of taxation can attract businesses to India?
2. Explain the advantages and disadvantages of such tax reforms.

Public Sector Policy

Under the industrialisation-led growth model of development, the public sector in India entered into almost every conceivable area of productive activity. Many public-sector enterprises were highly inefficient; indeed, they were little more than guarantors of continuous employment to some workers. In 1997, for example, the Bureau of Public Enterprise calculated that public-sector enterprises as a whole, representing a total capital worth of Rs 600 billion, were earning a negative real rate of return.

Public-sector restructuring policy took the form of selective disinvestment rather than privatisation per se. Initially, the government retained 51 per cent of the equity and, therefore, control over management. This percentage has subsequently been lowered in some areas. Revenues from disinvestment have been used for general budgetary purposes. Public sector undertakings were given the clear signal that their investment plans would have to be financed either by internal resource generation or through the capital markets.

Although the budget constraints of loss-making enterprises have become much harder, the government has not ordered any public-sector enterprise to be closed, but has brought public-sector undertakings under the purview of the Board of Industrial and Financial Reconstruction to facilitate their restructuring. The Board deals with companies and public sector undertakings in poor financial and commercial condition.

Agricultural Sector Reforms

Under the Indian Constitution, agriculture is within the purview of the states. Thus, the strategy adopted by the Central Government of lowering the budget deficit by reducing the transfers to the states has meant that investment (both public and private) in agriculture has stagnated.

In contrast, the lowering of the protection for the industry and the end of the overvaluation of the rupee have reduced the anti-agriculture bias in India's development strategy.

Agricultural exports have become viable, particularly those from the agro-processing industry. All Central Government restrictions on inter-state trade in food grains have been removed, although some State Government restrictions remain. The procurement of food grains has registered handsome gains, leading to substantial increases in farm incomes. Agricultural credit markets are, however, a cause of worry. Laxness in loan recovery has made several cooperative banks non-viable.

Labour Market Reforms

Indian labour laws provide considerable protection from retrenchment to labour in the organised sector of the economy. These laws have reduced the impact of successes in other policy areas. Flexible labour laws are needed to attract new capital and to make old firms with a history of excess labour more viable.

Advocates of economic reform have argued that a successful long-term reform strategy should devote more attention to the sector that is slowest to change. In the Indian case, this is the labour market. Some flexibility has been transmitted through a voluntary retirement scheme, but this is of limited help and is no substitute for a rational policy.

Complementary Social Measures

From the very beginning policy planners recognised that, while market-oriented economic reforms would improve investment and growth prospects, these could not be looked upon as ends in themselves, given India's mammoth and long-standing problems of inequality and poverty.

The government was aware that the reform and structural adjustment programme would result in a temporary fall in public expenditure and that economic growth did not automatically 'trickle down' to the poor. Hence, a number of programmes directly attacking poverty were initiated. These included the following.

Fig. 2.4 'Food for Work' programme has helped to sustain local population in disaster hit areas

- The 'Food for Work' programme, begun in 1977, subsidised food supplies through the public distribution system and concessional loan schemes for on- and off-farm development for small farmers, marginal farmers and agricultural labourers.

- Other on-going initiatives have concentrated on the creation of rural wage and self-employment programmes through asset endowment rather than on needs-oriented programmes designed to ensure access to basic amenities, such as drinking water, to the underprivileged. The most prominent among these is the Jawahar Rozgar Yojana which brings together the National Rural Employment Programme and the Rural Landless Employment Guarantee Programme. Among these, the Maharashtra Employment Guarantee Scheme derives its success mainly from the strong political commitment of the state government.
- In addition, there are the Integrated Rural Development Programme, the Employment Assurance Scheme, the Accelerated Rural Water Supply Programme, and various area-specific schemes to combat endemic poverty caused by hostile agro-climatic conditions and the degeneration of the ecosystem.
- A National Renewal Fund was set up in February 1992 to provide assistance to workers becoming redundant due to the adjustment programme. This fund was expected to finance the retraining, redeployment and retrenchment of the workers.

Focus

Economic reforms in a nutshell

- Tariffs were reduced from an average of 85 per cent to 25 per cent of import value.
- The rupee became convertible.
- By the mid-1990s, total foreign trade, i.e. imports plus exports, amounted to more than 20 per cent of GDP.
- Foreign Direct Investment (FDI) was encouraged and grew from effectively zero in the 1980s to $5 billion a year by the mid-1990s.
- Encouragement of foreign investment provided automatic government approval for FDI joint ventures in which foreigners held up to 51 per cent of the equity.

Aid to Learning

In view of the various reforms mentioned, explain the changing role of the State in the Indian economy since 1991. (Hint: Discuss the role of the State as a producer, regulator, planner-participator and facilitator.)

Although India has made significant progress in the second half of the twentieth century in comparison with its colonial past, poverty and deprivation persist among at least one-fourth of India's 1 billion people.

Regional disparity, poverty, unemployment and deprivation have created serious imbalances and India has to go a long way to transform its growth into development.

The Eleventh Five-year Plan recognised the need for sustaining post-liberalisation growth in the Indian economy. In his budget speech, Pranab Mukherjee, the then Finance Minister of India (and the President of India since July 2012), indicated a push towards greater financial reform, improved governance and economic liberalisation.

Fig. 2.5 Pranab Mukherjee with Hillary Clinton in 2011

Case Study

Eleventh Plan (2007–2012): A Move towards Sustainable Development
The eleventh plan has the following objectives.

1. **Income and Poverty**
    - Accelerate GDP growth from 8 per cent to 10 per cent and then maintain it at 10 per cent in the 12th Plan in order to double per capita income by 2016–2017
    - Increase the agricultural GDP growth rate to 4 per cent per year to ensure a broader spread of benefits
    - Create 70 million new work opportunities
    - Reduce educated unemployment to below 5 per cent
    - Raise real wage rate of unskilled workers by 20 per cent
    - Reduce the headcount ratio of consumption poverty by 10 percentage points.

2. **Education**
    - Reduce dropout rates of children from elementary school from 52.2 per cent in 2003–2004 to 20 per cent by 2011–2012
    - Develop minimum standards of educational attainment in elementary school and monitor the effectiveness of education through regular testing to ensure quality
    - Increase literacy rate for persons of age 7 years or more to 85 per cent
    - Lower gender gap in literacy to 10 percentage points
    - Increase the percentage of each cohort going to higher education from the present 10 per cent to 15 per cent by the end of the plan.

3. **Health**
    - Reduce the infant mortality rate to 28 and maternal mortality ratio to 1 per 1000 live births

- Reduce total fertility rate to 2.1
- Provide clean drinking water for all by 2009 and ensure that there are no slip-backs
- Reduce malnutrition in children of age 0–3 to half its present level
- Reduce anaemia among women and girls by 50 per cent.

4. **Women and Children**
   - Raise the sex ratio for age group 0–6 to 935 by 2011–2012 and to 950 by 2016–2017
   - Ensure that at least 33 per cent of the direct and indirect beneficiaries of all government schemes are women and girl children
   - All children to enjoy a safe childhood, without any compulsion to work.

5. **Infrastructure**
   - Ensure electricity connection and round-the-clock power to all villages and Below Poverty Line (BPL) households by 2009
   - Ensure an all-weather road connection to all habitation with a population of 1000 and above (500 in hilly and tribal areas) by 2009, and ensure coverage of all significant habitation by 2015
   - Connect every village by telephone by November 2007 and provide broadband connectivity to all villages by 2012
   - Provide homestead sites to all by 2012 and step up the pace of house construction to cover all the rural poor by 2016–2017.

6. **Environment**
   - Increase forest and tree cover by 5 percentage points
   - Attain WHO standards of air quality in all major cities by 2011–2012
   - Treat all urban waste water by 2011–2012 to clean river waters
   - Increase energy efficiency by 20 percentage points by 2016-2017
   - Extension and promotion of agro- and farm forestry in the farm sector
   - Improve air quality by reducing vehicular pollution and effective urban transport planning.

Activities

Based on the case study above:

1. Explain the major policy objectives of the 11th Five-Year Plan.
2. Explain how and why education and health play an important role in the sustainable development of a country.

Aid to Learning

1. Taking the various objectives of the Eleventh Plan into consideration, discuss how infrastructural changes can influence the achievement of goals in the health and education sectors.

2. Are the environmental objectives likely to have an impact on the other objectives mentioned in the plan? Discuss.

   (Hint: For these two tasks you need to compare and analyse the different objectives and use your critical judgement to reach a final conclusion.)

Exercise

1. What is meant by the term economic reforms? What does it include?
2. Why do you think the Indian economy opened up to foreign investments and trade?
3. What advantages and disadvantages do privatisation bring?
4. How can globalisation contribute towards India's economic growth?
5. Highlight some of the key economic reforms implemented in India with a view to improve the structure of the economy.
6. What initiatives has the Indian government taken in order to strengthen the 'trickle down' effect of economic growth?
7. In the light of the objectives laid out in 2007 during the Eleventh Five-Year Plan, research and assess India's performance.

Chapter 5 Economic Planning

Key Question

How is the policy of economic liberalisation in India best explained?

India: A Mixed Economy

The Indian economy is a mixed economy. It has acquired this form with the growth of a large public sector since Independence in 1947. The growth of the public sector was primarily an historical necessity. At the time of Independence, private enterprise had neither the resources nor the will to undertake the task of industrial development on a massive scale. Furthermore, the country's infrastructure was in complete disorder. At this juncture, the economy needed a 'big push' in the form of an effective intervention of the State alongside the private sector. The Five-Year Plans initiated since 1951 provided the basic framework for the economic development strategy of the country.

However, the private sector was allowed limited freedom in its operations. With the passage of time, more and more concessions were granted to the private sector to expand its business activities. But India stagnated until bold neo-liberal economic reforms were triggered off by the currency crisis of 1991. This was implemented by the Government of Prime Minister Narasimha Rao and the then Finance Minister, Manmohan Singh. This unleashed the current wave of rapid economic growth at a pace that promised to double the average productivity levels and living standards in India every sixteen years.

At present, a big segment of the industrial sector is in private hands. With the exception of some basic industries, all other industries including cotton textiles, jute, sugar, cement, leather, and information technology are in private hands. Though railways are still owned by the State, road transport and agriculture are completely in private hands. The private sector has delineated significant development in terms of investment and GDP contribution.

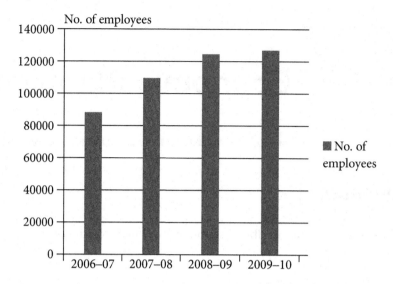

Fig. 2.6   Growth in the number of employees in new private sector banks

Planning in India

The Planning Commission was set up in March 1950 to promote a rapid rise in the standard of living of the people by efficient exploitation of resources of the country, increasing production and offering opportunities to all for employment in the service of the community.

The Planning Commission was charged with the responsibility of making assessment of all resources of the country, augmenting deficient resources, formulating plans for the most effective and balanced utilisation of resources and determining priorities. The state was

Fig. 2.7   Jawaharlal Nehru, India's first Prime Minister and Chairman of the Planning Commission

entrusted to play a proactive economic role in deciding about 'what, how, how much, where and whom'. This was to be done while respecting, by and large, institutions of private property and market.

The National Development Council is an integral part of the Planning Commission. It is responsible for reviewing national plans, recommending measures for the achievement of the aims and targets set out in the national plans and for building up resources for national development.

India's economic policy after its Independence from British colonial rule was largely influenced by socialist-based systems influenced by the central planning of the Soviet Union. Economic planning has become an integral part of the Indian economy for the past five decades. Unlike in the erstwhile Soviet Union, however, economic planning in India has been introduced in a capitalist economic framework.

While implementation of the plans is the responsibility of the governments at various levels, the Planning Commission has the major responsibility of formulating the five-year and the annual plans. The Planning Commission coordinates the development programmes of the Union Ministries with those of the state governments and integrates them into a single national plan.

Thus, planning is comprehensive and indicative, combining both forecasting and a policy-induced projection of economic activities. Several working groups consisting of economists, experts and administrators and task forces are also appointed for seeking inputs on various sectors.

Aid to Learning

1. Why do you think planning is a prerequisite for economic development?
2. What have been identified as the main aims and objectives of planning in India?

Focus

Important Features of Indian Plans
- Indicative – do not carry an element of compulsion or inevitability although there might be some regulation and regimentation of economic activities in the various sectors.
- Comprehensive – encompass all fields of economic activity and all the sectors.
- Socio-economic – concerned with social as well as economic effects.
- Perspective – take a long-term view.
- Democratic – involve active participation and cooperation of the people.

In the first eight Plans, the emphasis was on a growing public sector with massive investments in basic and heavy industries. Since the launch of the Ninth Plan in 1997, the emphasis on the public sector has become less pronounced and the current thinking on planning in the country, in general, is that it should increasingly be of an indicative nature.

Profile

Dr Manmohan Singh

India's fourteenth Prime Minister, Dr Manmohan Singh, is rightly acclaimed as a thinker and a scholar. He is well regarded for his diligence and his academic approach to work as well as for his approachability and unassuming demeanour. In what was to become the turning point in the economic history of independent India, Dr Singh spent five years between 1991 and 1996 as India's Finance Minister. His role in ushering in a comprehensive policy of economic reforms is now recognised worldwide. In the popular view, that period is inextricably associated with the persona of Dr Singh.

Fig. 2.8   Dr Manmohan Singh

Planning Objectives

Indian planning works within a basic framework of objectives which are the guiding principles of each development plan. These basic objectives are listed below.

- **Economic growth:** To raise the standard of living by raising the per capita incomes has been the basic objective of the development planning in India. The target growth rate and the actual growth rates are indicated in the case study provided later.
- **Modernisation:** The second most important objective is to modernise the economy through structural and institutional changes. A fundamental aspect of modernisation consists in using technology and innovation to increase efficiency by upgrading quality, reducing costs, increasing the productivity of labour and other resources.
- **Self-reliance:** Till the third plan, Indian economic planning emphasised progressively reducing and ultimately eliminating the dependence on foreign aid and imports. This necessitated import substitution and expansion and diversification of exports. Since July 1991, the emphasis has moved to an 'outward orientation'.
- **Social Justice:** To render social justice to all, more particularly landless agricultural labourers, artisans, members of scheduled castes and scheduled tribes, women, and children. This included programmes to reduce inequalities of income.

Case Study

Objectives of recent Five-Year Plans

Eighth Five-Year Plan (1992–1997)

The main objectives were modernisation of industries, generation of adequate employment, containment of population growth, universalisation of elementary education and provision of safe drinking water and primary health care facilities. They also included growth and diversification of agriculture to achieve self-sufficiency in food and generate surpluses for exports, and strengthening the infrastructure.

Ninth Five-Year Plan (1997–2002)

The main objectives were agriculture and rural development, food and nutritional security, empowerment of women, accelerating growth rates, providing the basic requirements such as health, drinking water and sanitation.

Tenth Five-Year Plan (2002–2007)

The tenth plan highlighted the need for the reduction of the poverty ratio, an increase in literacy rates, reduction in the infant mortality rate, economic growth, increase in forest and tree cover.

Eleventh Five-Year Plan (2007–2012)

The major objectives were improved income generation, eradication of poverty, progress in education and health, better infrastructure, and a healthier environment.

Aid to Learning

1. Differentiate between planning objectives and the objectives of a particular plan.
2. Are there many common features running across the Indian plans?

Planning Strategies

The planning strategies that have evolved over the last fifty years of economic planning in India can be conveniently divided into two phases. The Phase of Control/Phase of Inward Looking Strategy started in the early fifties and lasted till the late eighties. This phase of strategy involved a mix of State intervention, expansion of the public sector, nationalisation, import substitution, development of heavy industries and self-reliance. This phase came to be known as 'licence-permit-quota raj' (investment, industrial and import licensing) as the State influenced much of the economic activities of the private sector through various controls such as licences.

Focus

Inward looking strategy at a glance

- Expansion of the public sector
- Industrialisation and import substitution
- Self-sufficiency in food grain production
- State control over financial resources
- Control of foreign capital
- Protection of small scale industries
- Regulation of large scale industries
- Curb on monopolistic practices
- Security to labour
- Provision of public health measure and spread of education and literacy.

The second phase of strategic planning was the Phase of Deregulation/Phase of Liberalisation, Privatisation and Globalisation/Phase of Outward Looking and it has been in practice from 1991 onwards.

Focus

Outward oriented strategy at a glance

- Export promotion and increased liberalisation in trade
- Increased Foreign Direct Investment (FDI)
- Increased competition for domestic industries
- Reduction in the role of Public Sector.

In early 1991, the worst economic crisis since Independence hit India. It was caused by

- Large fiscal deficits due to the widening gap between revenue and expenditure of the government
- Large deficits in the balance of payments and huge borrowings from abroad
- High inflation.

The crisis of 1991: A brief historical account

External shocks

- Middle East crisis and breakdown of the Soviet Union
- Increase in the value of oil imports in India due to a rise in world oil prices
- Deterioration in the trade account and an increase in the balance of payments deficit
- Loss of export markets, slowdown in export growth.

Internal shocks

- Political uncertainties and low investor confidence
- Widening current account imbalances and reserve losses
- Downgrading of India's credit rating by the credit rating agencies.

Exercise

1. What is meant by a development strategy?
2. Differentiate between inward and outward strategies.
3. India is a mixed economy. Discuss how this statement best describes economic planning in India in 1990. How are things different by 2012?
4. Differentiate between planning objectives and planning strategies.
5. Define the following terms:
    (a) Fiscal deficit
    (b) Export promotion
    (c) Import substitution
    (d) Foreign direct investment
    (e) Self-reliance

Chapter 6   Impact of Liberalisation

Key Question

How far has economic liberalisation changed India?

The post-reform economic policies have helped build a lot of confidence amongst the planners to make further policy changes without disruption. These changes included devaluation, trade liberalisation and de-licensing of investment to spur growth. However, it is questionable, for example, whether the July 1991 package would have been politically acceptable in the absence of the experience and confidence in liberal policies acquired in the 1980s.

Foreign Trade and Balance of Payments

Trade liberalisation had a much more visible effect on external trade in the 1990s than in the 1980s. The ratio of total export of goods and services to the GDP in India doubled from 7 per cent in 1990 to 14 per cent in 2000. The rise was less dramatic on the import side. This was due to the fact that increased external borrowing was still financing a large proportion of imports in 1990, unlike in 2000. But it was still a significant rise from 10 per cent in 1990 to 16.6 per cent in 2000. Within ten years, the ratio of total goods and services trade to the GDP rose from 17 per cent to 30.6 per cent.

Fig. 2.9   Indian exports doubled due to liberalisation

One of the key macroeconomic objectives of any government is to maintain balance in its external accounts (balance of payments) and in order to do so foreign trade policies are modified from time to time. Due to the liberal import policy, removal of all quantitative restrictions and reduction of import tariffs resulted in a deepening of the adverse trade deficit. The rise in the price of crude oil also led to a sharp increase in imports.

Industries

Many countries comprising industrial market economies, the former socialist economies and a large number of developing countries belonging to Asia, Africa and Latin America have launched massive programmes of privatisation during the last two or three decades or so.

The Indian Government's change of attitude was clearly demonstrated in the New Industrial Policy of 1991. The government adopted the route of disinvestment, did away with investment licensing, ended the public sector monopoly in many sectors and initiated a policy of automatic approval for foreign direct investment up to 51 per cent.

However, the most disappointing aspect of the 1990s experience has been the lack of acceleration of growth in the industrial sector. The average annual rate of growth in this sector was 6.8 per cent during 1981–1991 and 6.4 per cent during 1991–2001. Given that many of the reforms were particularly aimed at this sector, this outcome is indeed disappointing. There are at least three complementary reasons behind this.

Firstly, due to draconian labour laws, industry in India is increasingly outsourcing many of its activities. As a result, the growth in industry is actually being measured in terms of the growth in services. Secondly, due to some key binding constraints in areas of labour, small-scale industry reservation and power, large-scale firms are still unable or unwilling to enter the market. Finally, large fiscal deficits continue to 'crowd out private investment'.

GDP Growth, Employment and Poverty

The policy of LPG successfully proved to be the means of acceleration in the growth process. Although growth rates picked up and averaged around 7 per cent, there have been years when the annual growth rates have decelerated, making the growth process uneven.

Although the GDP growth rate was quite high, it did not result in a corresponding decline in poverty. The most important reason behind this contrast is the slowdown of growth in employment. Not only is the record in terms of increasing unemployment rates glaring, but their impact on labour is even more adverse. The liberal attitude of the government pushed labour from secure to insecure employment, increasing employers' militancy and weakening trade unions.

Performance of Public Sector Enterprises

The performance of the much maligned public enterprises and, more importantly, that of the central government PSUs showed distinct improvement. Till 1998–1999, the government used to sell minority stakes through the domestic or international issue of shares. Post 1999–2000, there has been a greater emphasis on strategic sale, involving an effective transfer of control and management to a private equity.

The prominent companies liberalised by such sales include BALCO, VSNL, ITDC Hotels, IPCL and Maruti Udyog Ltd. In addition to significant contribution towards the growth of the Indian economy, most of the public sector enterprises have been able to ensure viable operations on a self-sustainable basis.

Foreign Investment Inflows

A major objective of the economic reforms was to increase capital formation of the economy without creating foreign debt. Foreign investment flows take two forms, namely foreign direct investment and portfolio investment. As against the FDI, the foreign portfolio investment has shown violent fluctuations. Consequently, this has become an undependable source of foreign funds. However in comparison to India, China has been able to attract a much higher level of foreign investment. The Indian Government is continuously striving to remove the hurdles in the path of foreign investors in order to maximise FDI inflows.

Foreign Direct Investment (FDI)

The foreign direct investment is profitable both to the country receiving investment and the investor. In order to attract foreign capital and investments from non-resident Indians, the government has in recent years announced a number of tax concessions and lower rates of taxation for certain priority industries. With the announcement of the New Industrial Policy in July 1991, the FDI was allowed to flow freely in all sectors including the services sector. While the approvals witnessed a rapid increase, the actual inflows were much less.

Aid to Learning

1. Look closely at the various growth indicators over the last five years given on p-67. Now write a detailed report titled 'India's growth performance.'

   (Hint: You have to pay close attention to the figures in the graphs and take into account the changing trends from one year to the next.)

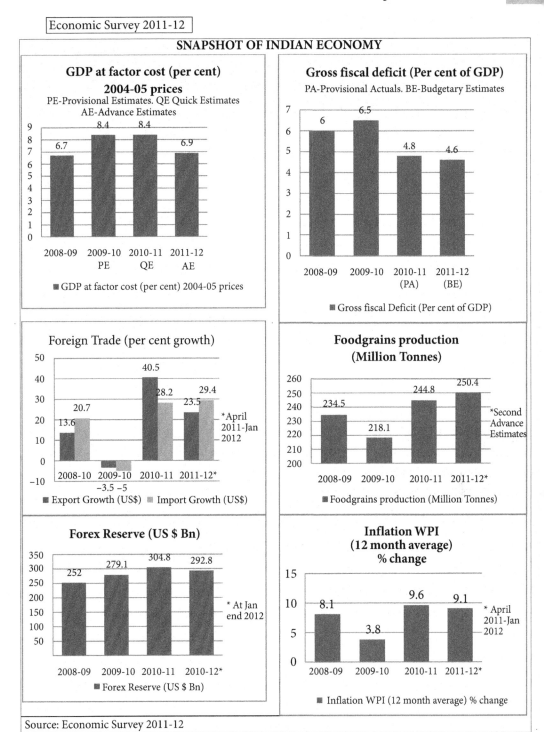

Economic Survey 2011-12

SNAPSHOT OF INDIAN ECONOMY

GDP at factor cost (per cent)
2004-05 prices
PE-Provisional Estimates. QE Quick Estimates
AE-Advance Estimates

GDP at factor cost (per cent) 2004-05 prices

Gross fiscal deficit (Per cent of GDP)
PA-Provisional Actuals. BE-Budgetary Estimates

Gross fiscal Deficit (Per cent of GDP)

Foreign Trade (per cent growth)

*April 2011-Jan 2012

Export Growth (US$)   Import Growth (US$)

Foodgrains production
(Million Tonnes)

*Second Advance Estimates

Foodgrains production (Million Tonnes)

Forex Reserve (US $ Bn)

* At Jan end 2012

Forex Reserve (US $ Bn)

Inflation WPI
(12 month average)
% change

* April 2011-Jan 2012

Inflation WPI (12 month average) % change

Source: Economic Survey 2011-12

Fig. 2.10   The various growth indicators over the last five years

Table 2.2   FDI inflows by source country

Rank	Country	FDI projects			Change 2011 vs. 2010	Value (US$ million 2011	Job creation 2011
		2010	2011	Share in FDI 2011			
1	US	218	277	30%	27%	3,636	73,550
2	Japan	88	115	12%	31%	7,634	46,510
3	UK	85	87	9%	2%	2,672	17,202
4	Germany	81	87	9%	7%	1,877	13,466
5	France	30	32	3%	7%	4,166	17,710
6	Sweden	7	27	3%	286%	2,665	8,148
7	Switzerland	27	26	3%	−4%	1,164	9,810
8	Spain	23	24	3%	4%	984	5,686
9	UAE	17	23	2%	35%	944	4,871
10	Finland	8	17	2%	113%	828	3,102
11	Others	190	217	23%	14%	21,691	55,358
	Total	774	932	100%	20%	58,261	255,416

Source: FDI Intelligence

Aid to Learning

1. Analyse the data given in Table 2.2 and discuss the extent to which the FDI inflows are responsible for India's economic growth in the recent years.
2. Pick any two countries from the list above which are major contributors to FDI in India. Compare and contrast their role in the light of the evidence provided.
3. Look up the following websites to learn more about the FDI inflows in India:
   http://www.fdiintelligence.com/
   http://www.fdimarkets.com/

Small Scale Industries

Consequent to the unveiling of the new economic policies, a separate set of policy measures were introduced for the promotion and strengthening of the Small Scale Industries (SSI) in August, 1991. The policy proposed to impart more vitality and growth impetus to the sector in order to facilitate its contribution to growth in output, employment and exports. The sector was substantially de-licensed and investment limits in plant and machinery were increased. Further efforts were made to de-regulate and de-bureaucratise the sector.

However, the performance of the SSI sector indicates that it is facing a tough challenge for its survival and growth in the period of globalisation. The growth and contribution of the SSI have not been very impressive in the post-reform period. New initiatives are needed from the government.

Infrastructure Growth

Liberalisation has also had a significant effect on growth in some of the key parts of the services sector. Overall, the average annual growth rate in the services sector shifted from 7 per cent during 1981–1991 to 8 per cent during 1991–2001. This was mostly due to the fast growth in communication, financial, business and community services. Given the substantial de-regulation and opening up to private participation in at least the first three of these sectors, the link between this acceleration and the reforms can hardly be denied.

The telecommunications sector has opened up significantly to the private sector, including foreign investors. Until the early 1990s, this sector was a state monopoly. In 1994, the National Telecommunications Policy provided for the opening of cellular as well as basic and value-added telephone services to the private sector. Foreign investors were also granted entry. Rapid changes in technology led to the adoption of the New Telecom Policy in 1999 which provides the current policy framework.

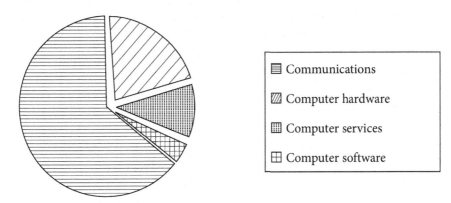

Fig. 2.11   Distribution of total ICT spending in India, 2001–2006

FDI upto 100 per cent is permitted in e-commerce. Automatic approval is available for foreign equity in software and almost all areas of electronics. 100 per cent foreign investment is permitted in information technology units set up exclusively for exports.

The infrastructure sector has also been opened to foreign investment. The FDI up to 100 per cent under automatic route is permitted in projects for construction and maintenance of roads, highways, vehicular bridges, toll roads, vehicular tunnels, ports and harbours. In projects providing supporting services to water transport, such as operation and maintenance of piers and loading and discharging of vehicles, no approval is required for foreign equity of up to 51 per cent. FDI up to 100 per cent is permitted in airports, with FDI above 74 per cent requiring prior approval of the government.

The Indian infrastructure offers immense opportunities for the private sector. Although the sector is booming, there are hindrances in the smooth development of world-class infrastructure. There has been a clear upward trend in the infrastructure industries such as steel and cement. However, other industries such as electricity, coal and petroleum have shown lower growth rates. The growth rate of coal has also declined and the sharpest decline has been noticed in the case of petroleum, despite the fact that FDI up to 49 per cent is permitted under the government route in petroleum refining by the Public Sector Undertakings.

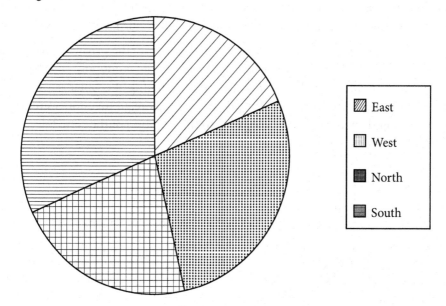

Fig. 2.12   Regional distribution of cement industries in India

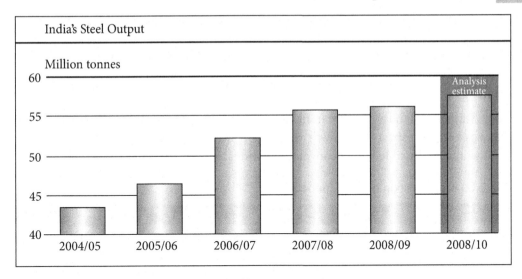

Fig. 2.13 India's steel output 2004–2010

Neglect of Agriculture

A major flipside of the economic reforms has been the neglect of agriculture, especially in terms of reducing the gross investment in irrigation by the public sector. The GDP in agriculture witnessed a decline in the growth rate as the reform process mainly had its emphasis on industry (manufacturing). This resulted in a decline in the output of food grains.

The poor performance of agriculture has been attributed to a decline in public investment in infrastructural elements such as irrigation and transport, a decline in farmers' subsidy and to greater competition from the international arena resulting from the withdrawal of support prices. Production for exports has reduced the domestic supply and has therefore pushed up the price of food grains.

Reasons for India lagging behind China

Sceptics in 1991 said that the reforms would fail. Clearly they were wrong. Nevertheless, it must be acknowledged that, in terms of its magnitude, the response of the economy has been substantially weaker in India than in China.

In China, the exports of goods and services grew at the rate of 13 and 15 per cent annually during the 1980s and the 1990s respectively. Imports exhibited a similar performance. Consequently, the fact of India's lagging behind, despite the systematic reforms of 1990s, can be explained in terms of the slow growth of conventional industry. This has a certain policy implication for India. India must free industry of its continuing restraints if it is to maximise the benefits of what has been done to date.

Indian industry cannot match the performance of its Chinese counterpart because of a number of reasons. These include a virtual ban on the exit, retrenchment and reassignment of workers, the continuing reservation of most of the labour-intensive industries for small-scale firms, and the absence of effective bankruptcy laws and continuing high protection.

In some ways, given the advantage India enjoys over China in the information technology sector, its overall prospects for growth are even better than those of China. But such a growth would be possible only if conventional industry is given a fair chance.

Table 2.3 Composition of GDP (per cent)

China			
Sector	1980	1990	2000
Agriculture	30.1	27	15.9
Industry	48.5	41.6	50.9
Manufacturing	40.5	32.9	34.5
Services	21.4	31.3	33.2
India			
Sector	1980	1990	2000
Agriculture	38.6	31.3	24.9
Industry	24.2	27.6	26.9
Manufacturing	16.3	17.2	15.8
Services	37.2	41.1	48.2

Aid to Learning

1. In what ways does India lag behind China and why?
2. Why is India compared to China?

Case Study

The Changing Face of the Indian Economy: Telecommunications
The telecom services have been recognised worldwide as an important tool for the socio-economic development of a nation. It is one of the prime support services needed for rapid growth and modernisation. The Indian telecommunication sector has undergone a major process of transformation under liberalisation.

The Indian telecom market has both public and private sector companies participating. The public sector has over 43 per cent market share, down from over 90 per cent in 2000.

- India is the fifth largest telecom services market in the world.
- India has a telecom policy that aims to encourage private and foreign investment. There is an independent regulator.
- Over 150 per cent growth in telecom services is projected in five years. This will require further large investments in network infrastructure.
- An investment opportunity of an estimated $22 billion is available across many areas such as telecom devices and software for the Internet, broadband and direct to home services, set-top boxes, gateway exchange, modem, mobile handsets, gaming devices, EPABX, telecom software, applications and content development ranging from gaming to education. Vodafone, Nokia, Elcoteq, Alcatel, LG, Ericsson are all investing in India.

Activities

Discuss in groups the role played by the development of the telecom sector in the development of any emerging economy like India.

Exercise

1. Study Table 2.2 and analyse any five major indicators of growth.
2. Identify some of the weak areas of growth in India. Suggest two measures that could overcome these.
3. What role does improvement in infrastructure play in economic development?
4. Explain the ways in which liberalisation has been a success in India since 1991.
5. Explain the drawbacks of liberalisation policies for India since 1991.
6. 'On balance, the liberalisation has not been worth the enormous trouble involved.' Consider this view of the period 1991 to 2012.

Human Development

To what extent have the human benefits of economic reform been too uneven?

Human development concerns much more than the rise or fall of national incomes. It is about creating an environment in which people can realise their full potential and lead productive and creative lives in accord with their needs and interests. People are the real wealth of nations. Development is thus about expanding the choices people have to lead lives that they value. And it is also about much more than economic growth which is only a means, even if a very important one, of enhancing people's choices.

Fundamental to enhancing these choices is building human capacities, in other words, the range of things that people can do or be in life. The most basic capacities essential to human development are to lead long and healthy lives, to be knowledgeable, to have access to the resources needed for a decent standard of living and to be able to participate in the life of the community. Without these, many choices are simply not available and many opportunities in life remain inaccessible.

Human Development Index for India

Each year, the United Nations Human Development Report publishes the Human Development Index (HDI) for all countries. This report looks beyond GDP to a broader definition of well-being. The HDI provides a composite measure of three dimensions of human development, namely living a long and healthy life (measured by life expectancy), access to knowledge (measured by mean years of adult education and expected years of schooling for children of school-entrance age) and having a decent standard of living (measured by Gross National Income, i.e. GNI per capita).

The index is not in any sense a comprehensive measure of human development. It does not, for example, include important indicators such as gender or income inequality and indicators that are more difficult to measure such as respect for human rights and political freedom.

India's HDI value for 2011 was 0.547 in the medium human development group of countries, positioning the country at 134 out of 187 countries and territories. Between 1980 and 2011, India's HDI value increased from 0.344 to 0.547—an increase of 59.0 per cent or an average annual increase of about 1.5 per cent. Table 2.5 below reviews India's progress in each of the HDI indicators. Between 1980 and 2011, India's life expectancy at birth increased by 10.1 years, mean years of schooling increased by 2.5 years and expected years of schooling increased by 3.9 years. India's GNI per capita increased by about 287.0 percent between 1980 and 2011.

Table 2.4 HDI composition for India 1980–2011

	Life expectancy at birth	Expected years of schooling	Mean years of schooling	GNI per capita (2005 PPP$)	HDI value
1980	55.3	6.5	1.9	896	0.344
1985	57.0	7.7	2.4	1,043	0.380
1990	58.3	7.7	3.0	1,229	0.410
1995	59.8	8.3	3.3	1,453	0.437
2000	61.6	8.4	3.6	1,747	0.461
2005	63.3	9.9	4.0	2,280	0.504
2010	65.1	10.3	4.4	3,248	0.542
2011	65.4	10.3	4.4	3,468	0.547

India's 2011 HDI is below the average of 0.630 for countries in the medium human development group and below the average of 0.548 for countries in South Asia.

Table 2.5 India's HDI indicators of 2011 relative to South Asia

	HDI value	HDI rank	Life expectancy	Expected years of schooling	Mean years of schooling	GNI per capita (PPP US$)
India	0.547	134	65.4	10.3	4.4	3,468
Bangladesh	0.500	146	68.9	8.1	4.8	1,529
Pakistan	0.504	145	65.4	6.9	4.9	2,550
South Asia	0.548	–	65.9	9.8	4.6	3,435
Medium HDI	0.630	–	69.7	11.2	6.3	5,276

Poverty in India

The Multidimensional Poverty Index (MPI) is a new measure designed to capture the severe deprivations that people face at the same time. It can be used to create a comprehensive picture of people living in poverty, and permits comparisons both across countries, regions and the world and within countries by ethnic group, urban/rural location, as well as other key household and community characteristics. The following figures show the components of MPI and comparison with selected countries on this basis.

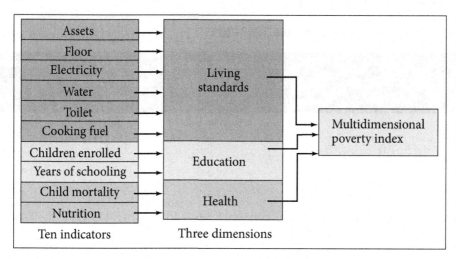

Fig. 2.14   MPI – three dimensions and 10 indicators

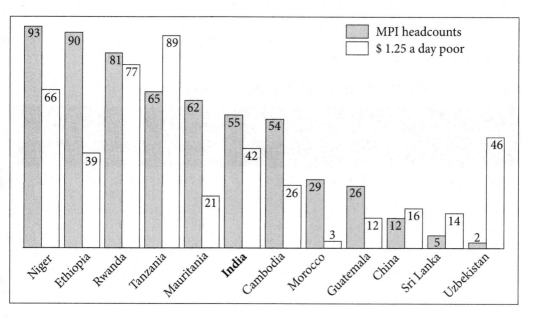

Fig. 2.15   Percentage of people living in poverty: MPI and income poverty

Activities

Facts on Poverty in India

- 81 per cent of people are multi-dimensionally poor in Bihar — more than any other state
- Poverty in Bihar and Jharkhand is most intense — poor people are deprived in 60 per cent of the MPI's weighted indicators
- Uttar Pradesh is the home of the largest number of poor people — 21 per cent of India's poor people live there
- West Bengal is home to the third largest number of poor people
- The multidimensional poverty is lowest for Kerala.

Source: A study conducted by Oxford Poverty and Human Development Initiative on MPI (2010) across twenty-eight Indian states.

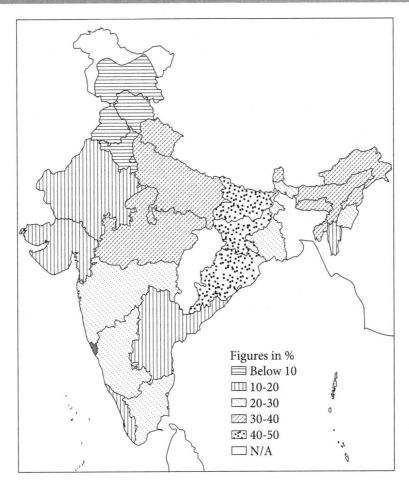

Map 2.1   India's poverty map 2009–2010

Emerging Issues

Poverty and Inequality

An important aim of economic growth should be the improvement of the living conditions of the poor. Economic growth that does not lead to sharp and sustained reductions in poverty may create new problems instead of solving them. Similarly, if rapid growth is achieved at the price of a worsening in the distribution of resources, it ultimately becomes unsustainable and engenders social tensions.

In India, the accepted wisdom is that the trend rate of economic growth was low and stable for a considerable period. A break was achieved through the process of trade and investment liberalisation and economic reforms initiated in 1991. This led to a sharp rise in the trend rate of economic growth. An important question that arises here is how this economic growth has affected levels of inequality and poverty in India. The approach to liberalisation in India (the Delhi Consensus) has some clear differences with the standard approach (the Washington Consensus). Of particular importance are differences in the basic philosophy of liberalisation.

India has opted for a gradual and controlled liberalisation and downplayed the stress on the speed of reforms emphasised by the Washington Consensus. In addition to this, there are differences in detail. Thus, apart from the IMF funds received in 1991, reliance on foreign bilateral or multilateral public capital inflows has been very limited. Consequently, after the reforms, policy-makers have been facing a hard government budget constraint but not a threatening external payments situation. The Delhi Consensus has emphasised the slow liberalisation of trade and a very gradual privatisation avoiding capital account liberalisation.

This prudent approach has sidestepped major shocks and the changes in inequality consequent upon these reforms have been modest by the standards of the transition economies. Rural inequality has risen at a slower pace than urban and the overall inequality.

The rise in inequality has been the result of three factors: (a) a shift in earnings from labour to capital income, (b) the rapid growth of the services sector with a consequent explosion in demand for skilled workers, (c) a drop in the rate of labour absorption during the reform period. There has also been an increase in regional inequality, especially in the incidence of rural poverty. This rise in inequality has implied that, despite better growth, poverty reduction has been sluggish.

India needs to look at inequality existing across the states. Special assistance and focus is required on states for poverty reduction and skills development.

Child Labour

There are more children under the age of fourteen in India than the entire population of the United States. As a developing nation, a great challenge for India is to provide sufficient nutrition, education and health care to these children. Children under fourteen constitute nearly 3.6 per cent of the total labour force of the country. Of these children, nine out of every ten work in their own, rural family settings. Around 85 per cent of them are engaged in traditional agricultural activities. Less than 9 per cent work in manufacturing, services and repairs. Child labour is a complex problem that is basically rooted in poverty. The Indian Government is implementing the world's largest child labour elimination programme, with primary education targeted at 250 million. Numerous non-governmental and voluntary organisations are also involved in this programme. Special investigation cells have been set up in states to enforce existing laws banning employment of children under fourteen in hazardous industries.

Fig. 2.16 Child labour often puts children in hazardous situations

Corruption

The extent of corruption in the Indian states was measured in 2005 in a study by Transparency International (TI) India. Corruption has been one of the most pervasive problems affecting India. It takes the form of bribery, evasion of tax and exchange controls, embezzlement and so on. The economic reforms of 1991 reduced the red-tapism, bureaucracy and License Raj that had strangled private enterprise and had been held responsible for the corruption and inefficiencies. Yet, the 2005 study by TI India found that more than half of those surveyed had first-hand experience of paying bribes or peddling influence to get a job done in a public office.

The chief economic consequences of corruption have been the losses to the Exchequer, an unhealthy climate for investment and an increase in the cost of government-subsidised services. The TI India study estimated that the monetary value of petty corruption in eleven basic services provided by the government such as education, health care, judiciary, and police to be around Rs 21 068 crores. India still ranks in the bottom quartile of developing nations in terms of the ease of doing business. Compared to China, the average time taken to secure the clearances for a start-up or to invoke bankruptcy is much greater.

Certain measures taken by the government have considerably reduced corruption, or at least have opened up avenues to redress grievances caused by corruption. One such significant measure is the Right to Information Act (2005). This and equivalent acts in the states require government officials to furnish information as and when requested by the citizens. They risk facing punitive action otherwise. Computerisation of services and vigilance commissions have also been effective in reducing corruption. The

Fig. 2.17 Computerisation of services has helped reduce corruption to a great extent

2006 report by TI India puts India at the seventieth place and states that it has succeeded significantly in reducing corruption.

Environmental Degradation

About 1.2 billion people in developing nations lack clean, safe water because most household and industrial wastes are dumped directly, without appropriate chemical treatment, into rivers and lakes. This contributes to the rapid increase of waterborne diseases in humans. Out of India's 3119 towns and cities, just 209 have partial treatment facilities, and only eight have full waste water treatment facilities. 114 cities dump untreated sewage and partially cremated bodies directly into the river Ganges. Downstream, the untreated

Fig. 2.18 Human habitation on the riverside pollutes water resources

water is used for drinking, bathing, and washing. This situation is typical of many rivers in India as well as in other developing countries.

Globally, but especially in developing nations like India where people cook with fuel wood and coal over open fires, about 4 billion suffer continuous exposure to smoke. In India, particulate concentrations in houses are reported to range from 8 300 to 15 000 $\mu g/m^3$, greatly exceeding the 75 $\mu g/m^3$ maximum standard for indoor particulate matter in the United States.

Key Question

To what extent, and in what ways, does economic growth have its impact on sustainable development?

The term sustainable development came into use in World Conservation Strategy in 1980. In the Brundtland Report of 1987, titled 'Our Common Future', it was stated that:

> Sustainable development seeks to meet the needs and aspirations of the present without compromising the ability of the future generation to meet their own needs.

Whether growth and development are sustainable in the long run is one of the most daunting issues that every economy faces today. The World Bank has long since recognised this and the annual World Development Reports of 1993 and 2003 are completely devoted to these issues. It is important for us to identify the commonality between growth and development which are based on using resources. Some, like human resources, are renewable and expandable, while others, like natural resources, are limited and non-renewable. Some of the areas of common concern are marine and riparian issues, trans-boundary environmental impacts, management of bio-resources, technology sharing and sharing of sustainable development experiences.

These resources are complementary and to a certain extent substitutable. The present day developed countries, in the early stages of their development, drew heavily on limited and non-renewable resources. In the later stages, fixed and human capital replaced an increasing amount of these limited resources. Sustainability of development therefore depends heavily on efficiency in the use of these resources and in their appropriate 'mix'. Providing economic growth to a growing population, while maintaining the economic output potential of the future as well as protecting the environment and conserving natural resources, is quite a balancing act for developing countries like India.

In India, in addition to industrial activity causing damage to natural environment, land use, water use, deforestation, forest degradation, loss of biodiversity, energy production and exploitation of non-energy materials have all resulted in environmental deterioration. All these have adversely affected the sustainability of India's development.

The sustainability of India's growth momentum hinges on resource security, particularly security of natural resources. There is a crying need for policy-makers to think beyond five years and develop a long-term perspective plan and strategy for the efficient use of natural resources.

Dimensions of Sustainable Development

- **Human Dimension:** Investment in health and education, especially for women, children and people in rural areas
- **Environmental Dimension:** Preservation of natural resources and use of environment-friendly processes and goods
- **Technological Dimension:** Use of technology that is safe for the environment and use of 'green' goods
- **Economic Dimension:** Use of state expenditure for reduction of poverty, inequality and unemployment and for the improvement of the quality of life

Aid to Learning

In groups, put the above points in order of importance. Then compare your list with those of the other groups. Discuss in class any differences between the lists.

Beyond Liberalisation

The liberalisation that was introduced as part of reforms by the end of 1991 did lead to a considerable expansion of exports in some sectors and a substantial improvement in the foreign exchange balance with a remarkable international response. Yet, the development performance of the Indian economy remains moderate combined with illiteracy, undernourishment, ill health, and social inequalities. The rapid expansion of these capabilities depend crucially on public action. This has been seriously neglected in India both before and after the recent reforms. Thus, India requires a strong reorientation of government policies in areas such as basic education, health care, social security, land reform and promotion of social change.

Any organisation, society or even nation without a vision is like a ship cruising on high seas without any aim or direction. It is therefore clarity of national vision that can drive people towards the goal. The first vision that was set by the generation of freedom fighters, under the leadership of Mahatma Gandhi, was a vision to achieve freedom. The unified and dedicated efforts of the people from every walk of life won freedom for the country.

Fig. 2.19   Dr A.P.J Abdul Kalam

The second vision was set under the presidentship of Dr A.P.J. Abdul Kalam towards the realisation of an economically, agriculturally and technologically developed India by 2020.

To realise this vision, the people of India have to build and strengthen their national infrastructure in an all-round manner. Therefore, adequate attention needs to be paid to the development of human resources together with their optimal utilisation.

To attain what is called the 'One developed India', specific roles have been identified for all the people: professionals, government ministries, public sector, private sector, small scale sector, MNCs, NGOs, and media. Alongside these, the following priorities have been identified for Human Resource Development:

- Improvement in primary and secondary education
- Empowerment of women
- Investment in science and technology
- Entrepreneurship development
- Increased role of private agencies and NGOs
- Improvement in the performance by government agencies and institutions
- Concern for the environment.

Aid to Learning

1. Why do you think is it important to empower women to attain the 'One developed India'? In what ways can women be empowered?
2. What do you understand by entrepreneurship development? What needs to be done to ensure that?
3. What are NGOs? How can they help in attaining 'One developed India'?
4. Is it possible to add to the list of priorities given? What would you add?
5. Would you want to remove any of the objectives from the list? Which one and why?

Conclusion

Although India's growth record in terms of GDP, increased Foreign Direct Investments, increased exports and expanding IT and financial sectors has given it the status of 'Shining India', there are a new set of challenges that call for a second generation of major reforms. Rising poverty, inequality, corruption in bureaucracy and environmental degradation are some of the challenges that India is experiencing. All must be tackled in India's next wave of reform if development is to be truly sustainable.

Activities

You are to advise the government on its priorities for the next Five-Year Plan. What should they be? What should be changed from the Current Plan?

Listed below are a few useful websites which can be referred to for information:

http://www.planningcommission.nic.in/

http://www.mospi.nic.in/

http://hdr.undp.org/

www.indiastat.com

http://www.unicef.org/infobycountry/india_statistics.html

http://www.worldbank.org/en/country/india

Exercise

1. To what extent is Human Development Index (HDI) a more effective indicator of development in comparison to GDP?
2. Identify the emerging issues that need focus in India's economic planning for future.
3. Define sustainable development. How is it different from the term 'economic development'?
4. How is poverty measured? What do the facts on poverty indicate about India's development?
5. "India needs a second generation of economic reforms." Explain why this is so.

Unit 3

Social and Cultural Development

Aims of the Unit

- Understand the role traditionally attributed to women in Indian society
- Identify the principal areas where women face discrimination
- Discuss the issues responsible for the problems faced by women in India and evaluate the measures taken to redress these problems
- Understand the rise and change in the position of the Dalits
- Explain why caste-based parties have developed and the reasons behind caste-based riots
- Identify the reasons for the growth of communalism and communal riots
- Understand why affirmative action is controversial
- Evaluate the effects of affirmative action

Key Concepts

Inequality: Occurs when a group in society is treated unfairly or not in the same way as the others. It could be social, political, economic or on the basis of gender.

Stereotype: A fixed and often wrong idea that people have about a social, religious, racial or ethnic group regarding how its members behave

Discrimination: When different groups are treated in ways that are different from the rest of the population as a result of gender, race or religion

Patriarchal: Related to a social system dominated and controlled by men upholding their values and views

Dalit: The term used to describe a group of people who used to be members of the 'untouchable' caste (the lowest in the traditional Hindu caste system)

Ethnic: Related to a group of people who have a common language and culture

Communal: Based on disharmony between two different (religious) groups

Affirmative action: A term for describing measures taken by the government, especially in the spheres of education and employment, to force change to help those who suffer from discrimination or subjugation

Positive discrimination: Particular groups, usually minorities, who suffer from negative discrimination, being given special treatment and opportunities to help them overcome their disadvantages

Time Line

1984 – Golden Temple Massacre

1984 – Assassination of Indira Gandhi

1985 – Shah Bano Case (controversy over different civil codes for different religions)

1986 – Muslim Women (Protection of Rights on Divorce) Act

1992 – Attack on Babri Masjid, Ayodhya

1994 – Criminal offence to use ultrasound technology for sex detection before birth

2001 – National Policy for the Empowerment of Women passed

2002 – Massacre of Hindus on a train at Godhra

2010 – Women's Reservation Bill (33 per cent reservation for ensuring seats to women in the Parliament and state legislative bodies)

Introduction

This unit focuses on four key areas of development and change in the social and cultural history of India. The first chapter considers the changing position of women in Indian society and examines how much progress has been made towards achieving gender equality. The next chapter delves into the long-standing problem of caste. It focuses on the scale of this problem and the extent to which it has been resolved. The third chapter deals with the dangers of communalism and the problems caused by the religious divisions in the Indian society. It takes into account the issue of the minority groups in India as well. In this, it deals both with the tribal and the religious minorities and considers whether their problems are being effectively solved by the government. The last chapter considers the question of affirmative action and whether positive discrimination is helping to solve the problems faced by women, the marginalised castes and the minority groups or whether, in fact, such action is actually making the problem worse.

India has suffered from inequality in a number of areas of life, be it gender or caste-based. The gender division may be understood to be natural and unchangeable, but changes have been made to the traditional perception that the main responsibility of women is within the family and that it only involves looking after the household and bringing up children. This perception is often reflected in the division of labour in many families.

The role of women in public and economic life has generally been very limited as men had been the only ones allowed to participate in public affairs and have been paid more than women for doing the same job. In many instances work done by women has gone unpaid.

Although changing attitudes is a slow process, women have become more politically active. This has helped to improve their position in public life and in the economic field.

The other major division is the result of religion and caste. This division is often seen in the field of politics. Although a secular nation, religious sentiments are an inherent feature of political life in India. It is a major reason for communal conflict throughout the period since Independence, particularly when it is expressed in exclusive and partisan terms wherein one group believes that its views are superior to those of another or when the demands of one group are formed in opposition to those of another.

Fig. 3.1 Women are becoming politically more active

Religious division is not unique to India, but caste division is. The caste system has created an extreme form of inequality in which hereditary occupational division sanctioned by rituals has been taken completely out of context. According to the traditional caste system, members of the same caste group are supposed to form a social community that follows the same occupation, marries within the same caste and does not eat with members of another caste. This system, based on exclusion and discrimination, particularly against the 'outcaste' groups who were subject to 'untouchability', has undermined the country's prosperity and prevented its unity. This unit shall examine how far this practice has been challenged by socio-economic developments within India.

Case Study

The 1985 Shah Bano Case

In 1978, a 60-year-old Muslim woman and a mother of five, by the name of Shah Bano, was divorced by her husband. Following the divorce, he refused to pay her maintenance under Muslim family law. She had no means to look after herself and her children. As a result, she approached the courts for maintenance and help.

The Supreme Court ruled that, according to civil law (Section 125 of the Code of Criminal Procedure) which applies to everyone regardless of caste, gender or religion, the man was obligated to pay for the maintenance of his family after divorce. It was not the first time that a divorced Muslim woman had been granted maintenance by the court.

However, Muslim leaders put pressure on the government to overturn the decision of the Supreme Court. They argued that the ruling of the Supreme Court undermined the right of the Muslims to be governed by their own personal law, in the same way that the Christians and the Hindus have their own respective personal laws.

The government, with elections due in the same year, gave in and passed the Muslim Women (Protection of Rights on Divorce) Act, 1986. Although Shah Bano was granted her maintenance, all Muslim women who were divorced after this period were not entitled to receive alimony from their husbands under the new Act.

The case brought a number of issues to light and caused much heated debate. The government argued that the decision was an example of the secular nature of the state. But the opponents condemned their actions and argued that the government was simply appeasing a minority

Fig. 3.2   Shah Bano

group. Critics argued that although personal law might apply to divorce, it did not apply to maintenance. They also argued that it was a clear example of discrimination against Muslim women, depriving them of the benefits of civil law. Most importantly, the law highlights the issue of the unfair treatment of women in India.

Activities

Imagine you are a lawyer representing Shah Bano and you have to draft an appeal to the Supreme Court explaining why the verdict is unfair.
- Think of the ways in which Shah Bano was treated unfairly.
- Consider the message that the verdict gives about the treatment of women.
- How would you argue that the government was wrong in passing the Muslim Women Act of 1986?

Now do the same exercise in reverse as a lawyer against the appeal. When you have done both, discuss in class the meaning of discrimination in India.

Aid to Learning

Discuss the question given below in groups.
- In what ways did the Shah Bano case illustrate the problems faced by women in modern India?

  Or
- Is her case unique to the Muslim women of India?

Chapter 8 | Gender Issues

Key Question

To what extent are gender inequality and gender stereotyping considered to be problems in contemporary India? To what extent is gender discrimination being overcome in contemporary India?

The Role of Women in India

India has been a largely male dominated society. This has had an enormous impact on the role and expectations of women. For many years women in India were brought up to believe that their main responsibilities were to do the household chores, bring up the children and carry out any unpaid work that was required on the family land. This work might range from gathering firewood and drawing water to farming, labouring and looking after the cattle.

Women were generally expected to work within the limits of their home, whereas men were meant to go out into the world to work and earn money. Although the Constitution of India promised women complete equality, it had not been realised despite dramatic changes in their legal, political, social and educational status. Women in India constitute nearly half of its population. According to the 1991 census, there were 40.6 crores of women as against 43.7 crores of men. The table below shows the amount of time men and women spend on particular jobs during the course of a day. This clearly indicates their dissimilar roles and expectations in as late as 1998.

Table 3.1 Hours spent by men and women in various activities

Activities	Men	Women
Income generating work	6.20	2.50
Household and related work	0.30	5.20
Talking, gossip	1.45	1.30
No work/Leisure	3.60	3.70
Sleep, self-care, reading	12.25	11.20

The table makes the following two very important points.

- Women do some work that generates income for the family.
- On an average they work an hour longer than men each day.

As the table shows, most women undertake some work outside their homes. However, in many instances, neither is this work valued nor are the women paid for it. When they carry out paid work, their efforts are hardly recognised. This is often reflected by the paltry wages received by women even if they do the same job as men. This is in spite of the Equal Wages Act of 1976. Women's paid work usually has little social insurance. They find it difficult to avail of childcare facilities and their health and safety are often put at risk.

In urban areas, women from underprivileged families work as domestic helps while those belonging to the middle class work in offices. Efforts to change the traditional roles of women have thus been noticeable and successful mostly in the urban settings rather than in the rural areas. Perhaps the most notable area of progress has been the IT software industry where 30 per cent of the workforce is women. These women are on an equal footing with men in terms of both their salaries and prospects.

Fig. 3.3 Occupational disparity among rural and urban women

Women's role in public life has been even more limited, despite the rise to prominence of women leaders such as Indira Gandhi. Earlier, only men had been allowed to participate in public affairs, vote and stand for public offices. The percentage of women in politics is still low, with never more than 11 per cent being elected to the National Assembly and less than 5 per cent to the State Assemblies. These figures imply that India has one of the lowest percentages of women active in politics among all the countries of the world.

It is in the rural areas that the differences between the roles of men and women are really acute. In some areas, progress towards gender equality has been very limited and women still play a very traditional family role. As a result, they are often imagined to be capable of playing only these traditional roles. Customary practice hence sets out gender-specific roles for men and women. This usually restricts women to their homes and makes it difficult for them to take on full-time employment outside the domestic sphere.

The promises made in the Constitution therefore remain largely unfulfilled since the traditional barriers are too strong to be done away with.

Aid to Learning

1. Summarise the differences between the roles of men and women in Indian society.
2. How closely does this reflect the pattern in your own family? Account for any significant differences.

Problems Faced by Women

Among the various problems pertaining to women in India, the most urgent ones are those concerning the issues of violence against them. This is exemplified by incidents of 'dowry burnings', rape, domestic abuse and sexual harassment both at home and at work. 'Dowry burnings' or 'bride burnings', as they are often called, occur usually when husbands and their families decide that the wife has failed to bring the desired amount of wealth to the family through marriage. The scale of the problem is so great that the National Crime Records Bureau recorded over 7000 estimated deaths caused by 'dowry burning'. But the reliability of these figures has been questioned as 'in urban areas 26 per cent and 22 per cent of all deaths in women were caused by fire-related injuries in age groups 15–24 and 25–34 years, respectively.' However, there are other equally important issues concerning women which are discussed below.

Education

The average literacy of women is 54 per cent, whereas for men it is 76 per cent. Fewer girls than boys go on to receive higher education after school. This is despite the fact that, in school, they perform just as well as boys. That said, 50 per cent of girls between 12 and 14 years of age do not get enrolled in any school. The average number of years a girl attends school is 2.4, whereas for boys it is 3.5.

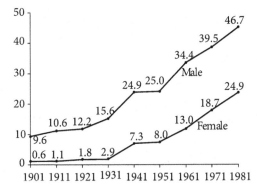

Fig. 3.4 Graph showing the wide gap between the growth in male and female literacy in India

Health

In India, the female life expectancy at 66.4 years is lower than that in many other countries, placing it 139/194 on the UN list. In rural families many women are victims of nutritional discrimination. Consequently, they suffer from anaemia and malnutrition. Maternal mortality in India is the second highest in the world. Contraception is not readily available to women, particularly in rural areas where sterilisation is the most common form of preventing unwanted pregnancy. A 1995 survey shows an all-India average of 34.2 per cent of currently married women as having been sterilised.

Similarly, female foeticide is another problem in India caused fundamentally by gender discrimination. Many parents used to abort the female foetuses, detected through pre-natal sex determination, because of their desire for sons rather than daughters. This practice was made illegal in 1994. But that did not prevent doctors from informing parents of the foetus' sex if they insisted on it. This has significantly affected the child sex ratio which indicates the number of girl children per thousand boys. The national average for girls is 927—a decline from 972 in 1901.

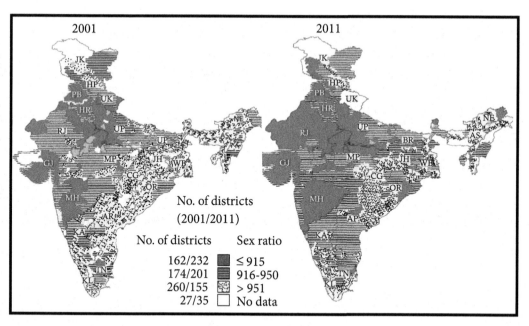

Map 3.1   Child sex ratio of girls to boys at ages 0-6 in 2001 and 2011 for the districts of India

This figure was 927 in 1991 but in some areas, such as Haryana, it had dropped to 865 in the 2001 census—a figure lower than that in any other country in the world. The 2001 census also recorded an all India figure of 933, but this figure dropped to 927 for the under six age group. The most important reason behind this drop was the abortion of the female foetus. As per the 2011 census, the total female child sex ratio in India is 944.

Legal Rights

The stigma attached to divorce is still high in developing nations such as India. There are a number of problems intrinsic to the levels of maintenance given to a woman after divorce as well as to a woman's legal rights to claim property. Earlier, most women did not own any property in their own names and did not get a share of parental property. But the 2005 Hindu Succession (Amendment) Act changed most of this. Some laws discriminate against women over land and property rights, as is the case with Christian women in divorce and succession cases. Despite the 1961 Dowry Prohibition Act, which made demands for dowry in marriages illegal, there is still much dowry related violence. A 1997 report claimed that at least 5000 women were victims of dowry death every year, and according to some figures there were 8391 reported dowry deaths in 2010.

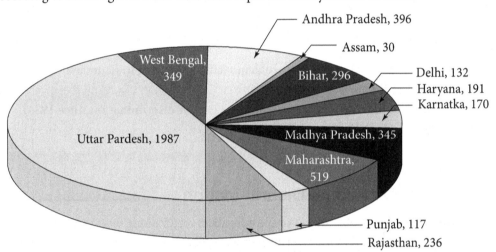

Fig. 3.5 Number of dowry deaths in Indian states

Aid to Learning

Draw a table like the one below.

Problem	Nature of Problem	Solutions if Any
Violence		
Education		
Health		
Legal rights		

Using the information above, complete the second column of the chart, summarising the problems women face in India today. You can complete the third column after you have read the next section.

Discrimination against women has at times been reinforced by the law and the legal provisions themselves. This is most noticeable in case of personal law, as we saw with the Shah Bano case. Personal law controls marriage, divorce, inheritance and the guardianship of children among other aspects.

The legal system recognises different personal laws for Christians, Muslims and Parsis. But other religious groups are governed by Hindu personal law. Women are often treated unfairly by the different forms of personal law in India. Most importantly, the personal laws of certain religious communities do not require marriages to be registered. This allows men from those communities to enter into bigamous relationships which can create further complications for women when it comes to divorce and separation.

Activities

Discuss the following in groups.

- What do you think is the greatest problem facing women in India today? Why do you think this to be the most serious problem?
- What measures have been taken to overcome gender discrimination since 1984?
- How successful have the measures been?

Measures to Overcome Discrimination

The opening up of new opportunities in the education sector along with political developments and new economic reforms have created a number of avenues for women's development, progress, security and self-realisation. The Constitution of India ensures gender equality as a Fundamental Right and also empowers the state to adopt measures of positive discrimination in favour of women by ways of legislation and policies.

However, whether these have succeeded in eliminating the problems pertaining to the issues of women's security, education, health and rights is a question that one needs to think about. The following discussion throws light on this question of utmost importance.

Violence against Women

Although the period since the 1990s has seen a significant number of laws passed to prevent crimes such as dowry burnings and rape, many argue that they have not been able to effectively solve the problem. The underlying cause of this violence is the assumption in Indian society that men are superior to women. As a result it is accepted that men dominate and control women, which for its part has led to the assumption that violence against women is normal and equally acceptable.

The type of violence varies widely, from verbal insults and humiliation to physical torture. But at its most extreme it has sometimes culminated in death. However, because of the structure of society, the violence is often hidden. The most common place where this violence takes place is the home—the very place where women should feel the most secure.

Aid to Learning

1. Why does violence against women mostly remain hidden? Who or what can bring it out in the light?
2. Can women themselves be active in addressing the violence against them? How?

Education

Education is a reasonably good indicator of development and the right of every individual to education is one of the first provisions of Universal Declaration on Human Rights. The attempt to improve the education of women in India has seen great regional variations. In many states, girls are still forced to drop out of school as families prefer to spend money on the education of boys. These families fail to see the benefits of educating a girl child since, as per established social norms, she is ultimately meant to leave home after marriage (although, in some areas, education is seen as a tool to improve the marriage prospects of a girl). Calculations made in 1990–1991 have suggested that the literacy rate of females is as low as 39 per cent and that half of all females in the 15–19 age group are illiterate, compared to 10 per cent in China.

In Uttar Pradesh and Bihar, 66 per cent of girls aged between 12 and 14 years are not enrolled in schools, whilst the figure reaches a staggering 82 per cent in Rajasthan. The figures are equally disappointing in case of age groups below 12. For example, only 42 per cent of those aged between 10 and 14 attend school. And for those aged between 5 and 9 years the figure drops to 40 per cent.

These facts and figures clearly show that there is still much work that has to be done to promote education for girls. Often, when a neighbouring village has an elementary school, the families are willing to send their boys there but unfortunately not the girls. That said, a different and more progressive response has been observed when schools are available in the close vicinity and teaching is regular.

However, the picture is not completely bleak. Many of the underprivileged are aware that education is the best way out of the trap of poverty. It provides opportunities that facilitate moving up in the social ladder and hence improving the condition of life. For example, the Indian state of Kerala has shown what can be achieved in the field of education. The adult literacy rate in Kerala has reached 86 per cent. This progress is also reflected in the female rural literacy rate which had reached 98 per cent for the age group between 10 and 14 years by 1988. At the same time, by 1993, 60 per cent of females aged above 6 had completed their primary education. The Government of India has recently launched the Saakshar Bharat mission for female literacy which aims to reduce illiteracy and spread awareness in the most remote and rural parts of the nation.

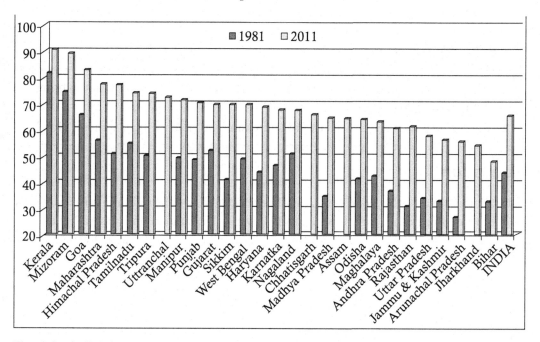

Fig. 3.6   India's increased literacy rate from 1981 to 2011

Health

As with many other issues, there are great regional variations as far as the question of women's health is concerned. For example, Kerala's female population with a ratio of 1058 is greater than that of Haryana where the ratio is only 861. Some studies have suggested that prenatal sex determination and selective abortion account for nearly the entire deficit in the number of girls born as second or third children.

Fig. 3.7   Campaign against female foeticide

More importantly, the studies have also suggested that selective abortion might explain the difference in the numbers of male and female first-borns. Technological development ushering in advanced ultra-sound equipment capable of revealing the sex of the foetus is one of the factors contributing to increased female foeticide. It has been estimated that over 10 million female foetuses have been terminated since the mid-1980s. However, pre-natal sex determination was made illegal in 1994 through the implementation of the Prohibition of Sex Selection Act.

Improvements in the economy and education have, however, not resulted in a corresponding improvement in the sex ratio. This is partly because there is a preference for male children. In both Hinduism and Sikhism, the religious rituals that a son performs for his parents after their death are considered to be very important.

There are also economic factors that have contributed to the lack of improvement in the sex ratio. As the state does not provide adequate old age pensions, sons are often required to provide for parents in their old age. The situation is worsened by the practice of giving dowry, which is still prevalent in many segments of the Indian society.

Politics

At every level in Indian politics, the system appears to favour men in line with the social constructs. It is usually men who are elected to most governing institutions. Although there have been some improvements in recent years, the gender gap in the political sphere is still very large. The highest number of women MPs elected to the Lok Sabha was 58 in 2009. This means that women constitute only 11 per cent of the total membership of India's Parliament.

However, women have benefitted significantly from the Constitutional Amendment Act of 1992 which gave increased power to elected municipalities and the village panchayats. In the local bodies and village councils, 33 per cent of seats were reserved for women. One third of the chief positions of the village were likewise reserved for women. As a result, a greater number of women were elected. This has, however, also created certain other problems. Political groups who represent the backward castes have started demanding that a quota of seats be reserved for women from these castes specifically. But they have not been able to get the Indian Parliament to change the 33 per cent reservation.

Aid to Learning

1. In which area of life in India have women seen the greatest improvements? Score each of the four issues (violence, health, education and legal rights) out of ten on the basis of the level of improvement. Explain your scoring with reasons.

2. Explain which of the following statements you most agree with about improvements in the position of women:
    (i) Progress in the improvement of the position of women has been slow.
    (ii) The most successful improvements for women have been in the field of education.
    (iii) The ideals of the Constitution are now much closer to being fulfilled for women.

Conclusion

Indian society has undergone significant changes since 1948 which have had an impact on gender relations. Although the promise of the 1950 Constitution has not been entirely fulfilled, it has become a benchmark for those pressing for greater equality. The institutions of democracy have and will continue to provide opportunities for more equal treatment.

The position of women in India is gradually improving. But it is a slow process. In the 1990s, a series of grants from foreign donor agencies enabled new, women-oriented Non-Governmental Organisations (NGOs) to be established in India. These NGOs along with the Self-Help Groups, such as the Self Employed Women's Association, have played a crucial role in the advancement of women's rights.

In 2001, the National Policy for the Empowerment of Women came into force creating an environment through positive economic and social policies to enable women to realise their full potential. At the same time, progress has been made on issues pertaining to sexual violence against women. In 2006, a Muslim woman was raped by her father-in-law and some Muslim clerics argued that she should marry him. But unlike in the Shah Bano case, the law prevailed and the culprit was sentenced to a term of ten years in jail.

Fig. 3.8 Kalpana Chawla

Fig. 3.9 Fathima Beevi

There is also a significant number of individual women who have become role models for young girls in India through their achievements. As early as in 1989, Fathima Beevi became the first woman judge of the Supreme Court. In 1997, Kalpana Chawla became the first Indian woman to go on a space mission and then in 2000, Karnam Malleswari became the first Indian female athlete to win a medal at the Olympics. The appointment of Pratibha Patil as India's first woman president and that of Meira Kumar as Speaker of the Parliament are some of the indicators of the progress taking place in the attitudes, ideologies and feelings of people towards women in India.

Activities

- You have just read about Fathima Beevi, Kalpana Chawla, Karnam Malleswari and Pratibha Patil. Find out about a few other illustrious Indian women from fields such as music, cinema, literature and fine arts.
- Find out about some of the recent initiatives taken by the Indian government for the sake of promoting women's literacy and empowerment.

Exercise

1. Why are women discriminated against in Indian society?
2. Why are educational and health reforms an important issue for women in India?
3. How serious are the problems facing women in India today?
4. How far has the position of women in India improved in the period from 1984 to 2010?

   (Hint: Use the following structure to help you.

   Introduction: In the introduction you should outline the problems facing Indian women.

   Paragraph 1: Education

   Paragraph 2: Health

   Paragraph 3: Legal rights

   Paragraph 4: Violence

   In each of the paragraphs explain the nature of the problems in detail, discuss the measures taken to solve them and comment on the extent to which these measures have been successful.

   Conclusion: Using the last sentences of each paragraph as your guide reach a conclusion as to how far the position of women has improved.)

Chapter 9

Caste in Today's India

To what extent is caste a problem in contemporary India? To what extent is caste-based discrimination being addressed and overcome?

Caste in the Indian Society

In the past, especially prior to Independence, caste had been an extremely crucial principle governing the structure of Indian society. It was hoped that with the coming of democracy this system would come to an end. But that has unfortunately not been the case. Caste continues to be a determining factor in the social sphere of India. Social communities are still formed by members of the same caste. The members of these communities marry usually within the caste and in some cases might have the same occupation. Caste imparts status to people depending upon their relative 'purity' or 'impurity' of origin as defined by the scriptures.

The lowest caste groups in the social strata were discriminated against in every possible sphere of life. They were the victims of the evil practice of 'untouchability'. However, the Right to Equality listed under the Fundamental Rights in the Indian Constitution put an end to caste-based discrimination, among others, in the post-Independence India. In addition to this, the Anti-Untouchability Act of 1955 made caste-based discrimination punishable by law. In fact, the word 'untouchable' has now been substituted by the word 'Dalit'. It is a Sanskrit word meaning 'suppressed or downtrodden'.

However, in spite of all the steps taken in the political sphere, caste continues to be a major problem in contemporary India. This was proved by the very need to pass the Prevention of Atrocities Act in 1989. It showed that the government was resolved to put a check on caste-based violence still rampant in India. The purpose of the act was to specify the crimes committed against the Dalits and to set out strategies and punishments for dealing with them. It outlined some of the humiliations that these groups continued to face including forced labour, denial of access to water and other public amenities and sexual abuse of Dalit women.

Despite the attempts to lessen its impact through measures such as affirmative action, caste still plays a subtle yet determining role in regulating Indian society. Some of the traditional aspects of the caste system are preserved and respected by people especially when it comes to marriage.

Discrimination on the basis of caste has not ended in the practical sense in spite of the constitutional attempts to put an end to it. Those groups or castes that did well under the old education system have been successful in acquiring modern education and the benefits that are associated with it, whereas those groups or castes who did not do well under the old system are still struggling to acquire a modern education in the new system. This helps to explain why there are more of the 'upper caste' among the urban middle class.

Positive Discrimination

Being an unequal system, the caste system has caused tensions in India over a long period of time. However, it took on a greater force especially towards the end of the last century. There were loud protests against the Mandal Commission's report which wanted to enforce more positive discrimination in order to provide greater opportunities to those belonging to the backward castes. At the same time, the period also saw extreme violence against the most backward castes.

Fig. 3.10   Road block to protest against the Mandal Commission

In an attempt to remove the divisions created by caste, their enumeration has been removed from the census. This period has also witnessed the Dalits as well as the other disadvantaged tribes gaining recognition and receiving positive discrimination in the fields of education and employment. However, this very process has also created friction and violence as other groups have voiced their objections to positive discrimination.

It is truly noteworthy how the backward and oppressed castes have increased their political influence and how the Dalits have learned to become assertive. The Mandal report had already recommended reservation of 27 per cent of all government jobs for the members of Other Backward Classes (OBCs). But when it was proposed, in 1989, that the government should implement this policy, members of the 'upper castes' were outraged.

Many middle class urban workers reacted likewise. These groups were anxious about their positions as it would add to the 22.5 per cent seats already reserved for the Scheduled Castes (SC) and the Scheduled Tribes (ST). However, the report was finally implemented in 1993. It is a clear indication of the progress made by the OBCs. Despite these developments, the issue has not been fully resolved.

Political parties have been looking out to appease the OBCs, aware of the votes that they could thus earn. However, in 2006, further trouble followed a proposal by the government suggesting that 27 per cent of seats be set aside for OBCs in educational institutions under the control of the central government. As with the Mandal Report proposals, there were concerns that it would undermine the position of the 'upper castes' and run counter to the ethos and standards of some of the prestigious educational institutions.

National Backward Classes Commission

The implementation of the Mandal Report had caused such a controversy that in November 1992 it was recommended that a National Backward Classes Commission be established. This finally happened with the passing of a Parliamentary Act in 1993. Its function was to determine the claims of the castes for 'backward' status.

It obviously raises the question as to why groups would want to be classed as 'backward' castes. But it is a clear indication of the benefits that were available, should one be granted the 'backward' status. This is supported by the number of applications for 'backward status' the Commission received.

In the period from 1993 to 2003 there were 1133 applications for 'backward' status out of which 682 were accepted and 451 rejected. The scale of the applications suggest that the applicants were acutely conscious of the benefits that came with the 'backward' status. This is further supported by the Commission's decision that the children of high government officials and people with an income of over Rs 100 000 per year would not be considered for being granted the 'backward' status. Despite these limitations, the number of applicants continued to increase and the income threshold had to be raised to Rs 250 000 in 2004.

The Rise of the Dalits

During the period before 1984, the Dalits had become increasingly assertive and active in politics. Although the Indian Constitution promises equality, this has not always been evident in practice. As a result, some Dalit groups became increasingly militant and the period saw the emergence of groups such as the Dalit Panthers.

These groups have put increased pressure on the government to implement state policy and they have also been able to force political parties to change as the Dalits have given their support to parties that favour them. At the same time, they have also become more self-confident. This is reflected in the self-assertive use of the term 'Dalit' and in the emergence of Dalit literature. This has helped to overcome the many divisions that have existed between the different groups among the erstwhile 'untouchables'.

Fig. 3.11   Statue of Dr B. R. Ambedkar

The unity among the Dalits means that they are not easily intimidated by anything and are able to stand up for themselves. This was proved by the incident in Mumbai in July 1997, when the vandalisation of the statue of Dr Ambedkar, the man who upheld the term 'Dalit', resulted in violent protests and riots. It caused the police to open fire and eleven people were killed. Attacks on statues of Dr Ambedkar were quite common during the period of 2000–2004, with over 500 such attacks reported. But the Dalits' aggressive retaliation every time proved their increased self-confidence and assertiveness.

Activities

- Construct a spider diagram to show the ways in which caste still affects the lives of many in India.
- For each issue you have identified, what are the problems?
- If you were a government minister responsible for reducing caste related problems, what action would you recommend to tackle each problem?
- What are the advantages and disadvantages of each of your solutions?

Emergence of Caste-based Parties

The passing of the Prevention of Atrocities Act showed that the problem of caste-based discrimination had been at least recognised and its enormity rightly understood. The Act established Special Courts to trail cases and also requested that states with high levels of caste violence appoint specially qualified officers to maintain law and order. Despite this, only a few states have created Special Courts. The Act has hardly been implemented, thus pointing at the problems inherent in overcoming discrimination.

The emergence of caste-based political parties implies these groups' desire for change and the failure, mostly of the ruling Congress Party, to respond to their needs. A good example is furnished by the state of Uttar Pradesh, where most of the top-level positions in the Congress Party were given to 'upper class' politicians. The same was true of the Congress' treatment of the Dalits. If they held positions within the party, they were rarely given anything that required real responsibility. They rarely held senior cabinet posts in state governments and were seldom elected as Chief Ministers. As a result, the Dalits started turning away from the Congress Party. This development has been reflected in the growth of new caste-based parties. The most prominent of these was the Bahujan Samaj Party (BSP) founded in 1984 by Kanshi Ram. It was also an indicator of the conviction of the 'backward' castes that social and political change was possible if they had a party representing them.

As a result, many members of the 'backward' castes became leaders of political parties. This can be seen with the BSP in Uttar Pradesh led by Mayawati and the Rashtriya Janata Dal (RJD) in Bihar led by Laloo Prasad Yadav. These new parties have been very important in the formation of national governments. Through this, they have been able to exercise greater influence on existing practices and hence bring about certain positive changes. Moreover, at a local level, caste-based parties have been in control of state governments, either as the sole governing party or in coalition, as seen in Bihar and Uttar Pradesh. This was observed most clearly in the 2007 election in Uttar Pradesh where BSP achieved a large majority. It was the first time that a party representing the Dalits had been able to break through the traditional pattern of coalition-based politics and form a majority government. It might be the first real indication for the backward castes to realise that they have the power to change their own situation.

However, despite this breakthrough, it should not be forgotten that in order to achieve a majority the BSP had to enter into an alliance with the 'upper' caste Brahmin voters. This reaffirms the fact that caste is still an important feature of voting patterns in India. It has taken a long time for the 'backward' castes to achieve a majority and this remains a serious problem. Although the Dalits have made great political gains in recent years, the government has by and large remained under the control of the political and social elites. Only by concentrating on national issues, such as price inflation and social and economic development, were the 'backward', caste-based parties able to win a majority. Moreover, it is important to note that in some areas of India the 'backward' caste parties have not done as well because of the majoritarian system used in elections.

At the same time, non-Dalit parties and some other groups have taken up some of the concerns of the Dalits, thus paving the way for further improvement of the latter's condition. This is supported by the agricultural labour unions set up by the different parties and NGOs. They have taken up issues such as wage demands, employment rights, right to work and education, housing and the ending of child labour. This has all helped to give Dalits an increased sense of self-confidence. The period has also seen the growth of exclusively Dalit organisations.

Activities

- Construct a chart to show areas of success and failure in improving the political position of the 'backward' castes.
- Make a list of national and regional parties in India and identify those which are caste-based.

Social Changes for Dalits

The Dalits have also been assertive in upholding the dignity of their women. This has been a major challenge as Dalit women face discrimination on three fronts, namely their caste, their class and their gender.

The reservation of seats in education and employment has had only a marginal impact at the higher levels. Very few in India receive higher education which gives them access to a government job. The chances of a Dalit benefiting from higher education are very limited since they tend to be financially underprivileged and come from under-developed rural areas. The reservation of seats in the legislatures has forced governments to take up the concerns of the Dalits. However, it is interesting to note a new trend that has come into being, namely competition between different groups of the Dalits. While the relatively better-off groups tend to dominate, the less well-off groups have started demanding further guarantees of representation.

There have also been a significant number of government schemes to improve the position of the 'backward' castes. This is best exemplified by the National Welfare Schemes which were designed to help the Dalits. The two most notable developments were the Mid-day Meal Scheme and the Public Distribution System. The latter supplies the poor and underprivileged with food grains at subsidised rates through Fair Price Shops.

Fig. 3.12   Children at 'mid-day meal'

However, the success of these schemes depends upon the class or caste of those running them. If those in charge are from a dominant caste, the chances of success are quite limited. In spite of this problem, governments have found ways to overcome the difficulties and have sought the help of voluntary associations. This has been particularly successful in Andhra Pradesh where women's organisations have helped with the Midday Meal Scheme and have ensured that the Dalit children actually received their meals. At first, this caused opposition from those of the 'upper' castes who withdrew their children from the lunches. But the government stuck to its guns and gradually the children returned, proving that if a government is willing to take a firm line then opposition and challenges can be overcome.

Caste and Economic Developments

Despite the actions of both the governments and the 'backward' castes, caste continues to have its influence over Indian society. There is much debate as to how economic development has helped in destroying the caste system.

Some would argue that industrialisation and the resulting urbanisation have played a major role in undermining the caste system. At the same time, in rural areas, agricultural growth has created rural employment and hence improved the condition of the Dalits. However, others would argue that at a local, regional and national level, the economic condition of the Dalits has not improved in spite of all the schemes that have been introduced. Hardly any Dalits own or have access to resources or control their own labour, employment and wages. As a result, they are still dependent upon the 'upper' castes for employment and can still be exploited.

However, policies such as rural employment guarantee schemes and rural income generating schemes, which include subsidies and loans for dairy farming and goat rearing, have helped to improve the situation. This has been further enhanced where the redistribution of land has taken place. In some states, such as Andhra Pradesh, Dalits have been able to purchase land through the provision of grants and loans from the government.

As a result, 'untouchability' has seen some decline in rural areas. But even greater progress has been made in urban areas. The demand for labour has meant that business has been unable to ignore the vast labour market that the Dalits provide. At the same time, the economic developments that India has witnessed since liberalisation have been to the benefit of only certain specific groups. In many cases, caste continues to define the jobs available and business networks that can be joined. The system of reservations has not been implemented in the private sector and therefore members of other 'upper' castes are at a massive advantage there.

Moreover, in smaller businesses, it is clear that family and kinship networks, which are still heavily caste-based, largely determine who is employed and what job they can do. It is noticeable that those from the 'backward' castes and hailing from rural backgrounds are less likely to succeed in what has become a very competitive market. The table below is a clear indication of the problems facing the Scheduled Castes and Tribes, with over 70 per cent of those living below the poverty line coming from those groups.

Table 3.2 Percentage of population living below the poverty line, 1999–2000

Caste and Community group	Rural	Urban
Scheduled tribes	45.8	35.6
Scheduled castes	35.9	38.3
Other backward classes	27	29.5
Muslims	26.8	34.2
Hindu Upper Castes	11.7	9.9
Christians	9.6	5.4
Sikhs	0	4.9

Table 3.2   Percentage of population living below the poverty line, 1999–2000 (Continued)

Caste and Community group	Rural	Urban
Other Upper Castes	16	2.7
All Groups	27	23.4

Aid to Learning

Consider the following statements.

- There have been far greater improvements for Dalits in the cities than in the countryside.
- Economic improvements for Dalits have been far greater than the political changes.
- The economic improvements for Dalits have not been extensive.
- Government action to improve the position of the Dalits has been unsuccessful.
- Dalits still lack access to many of the basic social necessities.

1. Which of these statements do you agree with? What evidence is there to support the statements?
2. Which of the statements do you disagree with? What evidence is there that undermines the statements?

Case Study

The Maharashtra riots

Despite attempts to stop inter-caste violence, it is still quite a common occurrence in India. This was shown most clearly in the murder of the four members of the Bhotmange family in September 2006. The Bhotmanges were Mahars, who have been more successful than most of the other Dalits. They belonged to the same caste as Ambedkar himself. Although the family was poor, they were doing remarkably well. The seventeen year old daughter had graduated from school and had also topped her class. Her success and prospects had angered the members of the Kunbi caste, who, although poor, were not Dalits. The indications of upward mobility earned the wrath of the higher caste villagers. To make matters worse, the daughter and the mother had identified in court those who had attacked a relative who had been campaigning to protect their land.

After the court case, a mob assembled at the Bhotmanges' family hut and great atrocities were committed against the family. They were taken in a cart around the village and their bodies thrown in different parts of the village.

Only Bhaiyyalal, the father of the children, could escape the deadly attack, as he was away from home. The police tried to cover up the incident, but Dalit youths began to protest for justice. However, the police turned against the protestors to stop the campaign. Then, in Kanpur, a statue of Ambedkar was beheaded. Kanpur's distance from Maharashtra not withstanding, Dalit riots broke out in Maharashtra, especially in Mumbai. Dalit youths attacked buses with stones. Then, as a symbolic gesture they stopped the Deccan Queen train, the epitome of 'upper' class luxury. Having stopped it, they ordered the passengers to get off and thereafter they set the train on fire.

This was the first time that Dalit youths had taken to the streets to voice their protest. The Prime Minister intervened and met Mr Bhotmange, who had been out in the village fields when the assault on his family had taken place. Bhotmange was promised justice by the Prime Minister. At the same time, police in Kanpur arrested a Dalit youth who had admitted to damaging the statue of Ambedkar in a state of drunkenness. However, others claimed that he had been framed for the offence. These people, for their part, took to the streets in further protest. The riots were eventually brought under control. But for the government it suggested that Dalit youths were becoming much more aggressive in their behaviour — a worrying development for the government.

Activities

Research the importance of Dr Ambedkar for Dalits.
- Why do you think that there have been so many attacks on statues of Ambedkar?
- Why do you think that his career is so important to Dalits?

The text suggested that Dalit youths are becoming more and more aggressive in their behaviour.
- Why do you think this is happening?
- What recommendations would you make to the government for preventing the growth of such behaviour? What are the advantages and disadvantages of each of your proposals?

Conclusion

Violent action against Dalits suggests that caste-based discriminations still exist, even if only in isolated areas. Fringe groups, such as the extremist militia Ranvir Sena, largely run and dominated by 'upper' caste landlords in the state of Bihar, have been established. They oppose the equal treatment of Dalits and take recourse to violence to suppress them.

Yet, these limitations to progress need to be weighed against the development of primary education and health facilities. These have enhanced the opportunities and the life expectancy for many, particularly when seen alongside the campaigns to end child-labour and promote literacy. There have been anti-poverty programmes, rural employment guarantee schemes and income generating schemes with provisions for subsidies and loans. These have helped the development of agricultural schemes for dairy farming and goat rearing. Housing programmes have also done much to improve rural life. This has been very important as it has taken away an instrument of control from the upper castes that earlier had the power to remove people from the land.

There have also been schemes to make land available, either through distribution by the government or by purchase through the help of grants. This is exemplified by the state of Andhra Pradesh. It has helped to put an end to the feeling of landlessness among the oppressed. As a result of these schemes, the issue of 'untouchability' has virtually disappeared from the urban areas, such as those in Tamil Nadu. Although it has seen a dramatic decline in rural areas, it is still evident in the heavily populated rural north. Compared to that, it has declined substantially in the more prosperous rural areas where increased employment has been bringing in wealth.

However, some of the positive steps taken by governments to improve the position of the Dalits have also created a backlash. There have been recorded attacks on Dalits by other peasants who are jealous of the gains they have made.

In any case, it would be fair to conclude that Dalits still suffer social discrimination, but 'untouchability', in its literal sense, is not there anymore. They have gained representatives in the Parliament. Reservations have ensured that they have jobs within the bureaucratic, police and public sectors. They even have their own political parties, with some ministers being Dalits themselves. The same is true of the other backward castes. Democracy has given them a great deal more of political influence. They are now able to demand even more quotas and are looking out to increase their share in the patronage that is available.

However, despite these gains, as Table 3.2 shows, the Dalits and some of the backward classes are the poorest in India. Their best hope of improvement is through education. Here the state has made some contribution to improving their position. But it is essential that this is taken further. Although the government has provided jobs through reservations, the area of growth will be the market economy and the private sector where there are no reservations. Unless this large group is educated, India's industrial growth will be slow as the country will not have the educated workforce required to succeed in the modern world.

The caste system is in a state of transition and is becoming less evident with India becoming a more liberal economic state. This development should continue as economic growth spreads into the countryside. Democracy has raised the status of the so-called 'lower' castes and they have been able to use their vast vote banks in elections to rise socially. There is a social revolution under way, particularly in the more backward northern states.

Activities

- Besides the various schemes implemented by the Indian government to empower the Dalits and the other backward classes, what else can be done to sensitise people to the need for getting rid of caste-based prejudices? Make a list of action points and discuss them in class.

- Refer to a few well-known Indian Dalits and find out if there have been any instances of caste-based discrimination in recent times. What steps were taken by the government in response to them? The following websites will help you in finding this out.

  articles.timesofindia.indiatimes.com/keyword/untouchability

  www.thehindu.com/opinion/lead/article699075.ece

Exercise

1. Why is the issue of caste still an issue in Indian society today?
2. Why does the issue of caste sometimes result in violence?
3. Why do you think that caste is a greater problem in rural rather than urban India?
4. How serious is the problem of caste in India today?
5. 'Government legislation rather than economic development has been the most important factor in lessening the problems caused by caste.' How far do you agree?

Chapter 10 Communal Tensions

Key Question

To what extent do ethnic and communal tensions weaken contemporary India? To what extent are problems of communalism being addressed and overcome?

The Growth of Communalism

Despite India's Constitution establishing a secular state, communalism and the development of communal parties are two very crucial features of the political scene in India today. It plays an important role in every election and is often used by parties to get people's votes. Over the last two decades there have been a significant number of communal riots. Some would argue that it is the greatest danger facing India today as it is a challenge to the secular Constitution and could in the long run undermine the country's unity.

Some of the most serious tensions in India since the 1990s have been religious in nature. This is best exemplified by the nationwide unrest triggered off by the demolition of the historical Babri Masjid in Ayodhya in 1992. Religious places have been the site of political tension and aggression from as early as in 1984 when the Operation Blue Star, undertaken at the behest of the then Prime Minister Indira Gandhi, led to the Golden Temple Massacre.

Regional conflicts too have often found expression through religion. However, it must be emphasised that supporters of communalism are not interested in religion; they simply exploit the religious sentiments of people to win support. It can be safely stated that religion is not the cause of communalism. The spirit of communalism runs counter to the values of all Indian religions. In order to understand the nature of the communal conflicts, it is important to grasp the essence of the terms secularism and communalism in the context of a nation.

Secularism involves separating the state from religious issues and making certain that it does not discriminate against people on the basis of religion. This had been the goal of those who drew up the constitution following India's Independence. Challenges to this constitutional ideal are therefore seen as a serious threat to the integrity of India as a nation-state.

On the other hand, communalism divides Indians into groups or communities according to their religion. It is driven by the belief that the interests of these communities differ socially, politically and economically. As a result, each group needs parties to protect their interests against other 'hostile' groups. It is the aim of those who support communalism to uphold the ideology of one religion or the other so as to have as large a number of supporters as possible.

The Causes Behind Communalism

It is often easy to identify the short term causes of communal violence. It could be triggered by a simple quarrel which can snowball into communal violence, if the feelings of the sides concerned have already been whetted and aroused by the political parties. Communal riots are the products of a sustained, seething and continuous discontent within people.

Communal violence often involves the urban poor who feel deprived, but whose numbers have grown dramatically because of the economic development. They live in over-crowded areas and have limited resources such as running water or health-care available. These people, given the difficulty and deprivation that their lives are beset with, are easy victims of those wishing to stir up communal hatred. Egged on by the latter, these people are ready to take revenge against those who might supposedly be responsible for their deprivation and poverty.

Fig. 3.13 Urban poor are easy victims of communal propaganda

At the same time, administrators have been somewhat reluctant to take serious action against communal violence. The State has the power but it has not yet acted in an assertive manner where the question of communalism is concerned. The State has also failed to prevent the spread of propaganda designed to arouse communal feelings, in spite of laws being available to prosecute those responsible for such propaganda. Lastly, but very importantly, secular political parties have often exploited communalism for their own benefit.

Some parties have entered into alliances with communal parties for the sake of gaining majority. This has given the latter a credible standing in India, making their communal ideologies almost acceptable. This fact undermines the very foundations of the secular State established in 1947. Secular parties have been willing to make concessions to religious groups as can be seen in a variety of incidents that will be studied in this chapter. It was evident in Rajiv Gandhi's decision to reverse the High Court ruling in the Shah Bano case and in his opening of the gates of the disputed site at Ayodhya in 1986.

Activities

Construct a spider diagram to show the causes of communalism.

Case Study

The Golden Temple Massacre

The Sikhs are a majority community in the state of Punjab. The Golden Temple, located in the city of Amritsar in Punjab, is one of the most sacred religious destinations for the Sikhs. In order to understand how and why the massacre took place, the events need to be seen in their broader political context.

Indira Gandhi had returned to power as Prime Minister in 1980. In order to keep up the support of the Sikhs, she had given hope to the Sikh preacher Jarnail Singh Bhindranwale that his political agenda would be seriously considered. His aim was the implementation of the 1973 Anandpur Sahib Resolution which called for Sikhs to be allowed to live in India free from direct and indirect interference.

Bhindranwale had made the Golden Temple his headquarters and by 1984 the compound and some of the surrounding houses had been fortified. Inside the compound, violent Sikh fanatics wielded submachine guns, resisting armed arrest by government security forces. Outside, the security men kept a nervous vigil, all too aware that the bodies of their murdered comrades may turn up in the warren of narrow streets around the shrine.

Fig. 3.14 The Golden Temple

These developments forced the government to act and the Operation Blue Star was launched to remove the violent Sikh extremists, who had taken cover in the temple premises. Shelling destroyed much of the outer defences, including the seventeen houses which Bhindranwale's followers were believed to have been occupying. Three main towers were also partially destroyed to remove observation points. Commandos were then sent through the main gateway of the temple. But they were all gunned down and those who managed to survive were driven back.

A second attack was more successful even though the commandos again came under heavy fire.

They asked for permission to fire back. But this meant firing at the Golden Temple which would have been an act of desecration.

At first the request was refused, but as reports of heavy casualties among the commandos came in, seven tanks were sent into the temple complex. They were able to clear the militants and the whole operation took twenty-four hours.

Fig. 3.15   Bullet marks on the wall of the Golden Temple

The Indian army had suffered 83 deaths. However, the incident recorded 492 civilian deaths within the temple and an additional 433 'separatists' were among the 1592 arrested. However, independent reports suggest that the numbers were far greater than those mentioned in the official versions of the whole incident. An Indian journalist reported, 'The government, after the operation, on the other hand, did everything in its power to cover up the excesses of the army action. The most disturbing thing about the entire operation was that a whole mass of men, women and children were ordered to be killed merely on the suspicion that some terrorists were operating from the Golden Temple.' As a result of the attack on the temple, some Sikh soldiers resigned and there were also reports of large-scale battles to bring mutineers under control.

The attack led to much criticism within India. Many saw it as an event planned before the temple was fortified, instead of its being the 'last resort' to remove the militants from the temple. The media blackout in Punjab meant that many did not believe the official government stories about the events and this resulted in widespread rumours. The timing of the attack also appeared to have been ill-advised as it coincided with an auspicious day in the Sikh calendar — that of the martyrdom of the founder of the Golden Temple.

Aid to Learning

The Golden Temple was attacked for a number of reasons. These might include:

- The temple had become fortified.
- It was a centre for militant Sikh operations.
- The government hoped to gain popularity from Hindu voters.
- The army was determined to crush the armed groups within the temple complex.

1. Try to put the reasons in their order of importance/significance.
2. What is the evidence that the attack on the Golden Temple had been planned for a long time?
3. What did the government hope to gain through the attack?

Activities

Discuss in groups why the newspapers would describe the operation as 'a greater victory than the win over Bangladesh. This is the greatest victory of Mrs Gandhi'.

The Assassination of Indira Gandhi

The consequences of the Golden Temple Massacre made themselves felt very soon. The massacre caused a great deal of anger and unrest among the Sikhs. This came to a head on 31 October, 1984 when the Prime Minister, Indira Gandhi, was assassinated by two of her Sikh bodyguards. No motive for the act was discovered. But it is believed that her assassins were Sikh extremists who wanted to avenge the killings at the Golden Temple.

Fig. 3.16   Indira Gandhi at a rally

Indira Gandhi had been receiving death threats ever since the massacre and it is said that she had remarked on the day itself, 'I don't mind if my life goes in the service of the nation. If I die today, every drop of my blood will invigorate the nation.' Her death unleashed a wave of violence across the country. Over the next few days, thousands of Sikhs were killed in retaliation.

The Babri Masjid

The Babri Masjid in Ayodhya too became the site and cause occasion of communal hostilities as well. In October 1990, L. K. Advani, the President of BJP which champions Hindu nationalism, led a group of Hindu nationalists on a *yatra* (journey) from Somnath to Ayodhya. Advani rode on a chariot, dressed in saffron.

Ayodhya had been the location of the sixteenth century Babri Masjid. But led by the Viswa Hindu Parishad (VHP), the Hindus claimed that the same land

Fig. 3.17   Activists on top of the mosque

was the site of the birth of Lord Rama. The Hindus wanted to reclaim the site and erect a temple dedicated to the infant Rama there. On 6 December, 1992, despite a government commitment that the mosque would not be destroyed, 150 000 turned up for a rally. Before long they attacked and destroyed the mosque.

The result was further violence, i.e. communal riots in many of the major Indian cities, including Mumbai, Delhi and Hyderabad. The communal violence caused over two thousand deaths and is considered to be one of the worst instances of communal aggression since the Partition in 1947. The riots in Mumbai lasted for a month.

The government's response was to set up the Liberhan Commission to look at the circumstances of the demolition of the mosque. The Babri episode is more than conclusive proof of the fact that major political parties exploit communal sentiments for their own vested interests. It further proves that India has a long way to go to overcome communalism, particularly when it is being used by political parties for their own gain.

Godhra and the Gujarat Riots

Talking about communalism and its relationship with politics in India, it is relevant to consider the case of Gujarat. A group of Hindus had been travelling to Ayodhya as part of the campaign to rebuild the Hindu temple. On their way, the train stopped at Godhra, where, according to reports, they abused Muslim workers. In response, 58 Hindu passengers of the train were burned to death in a carriage. Although the government enquiry was unable to reach a conclusion about the causes of the fire, there were some eye witnesses who claimed that a Muslim mob was present when it started.

Fig. 3.18   Buildings were set on fire during the riots

Gujarat's Chief Minister, Narendra Modi, reportedly arranged a mass funeral in Ahmedabad for the victims which, as many claim, was taken as the signal for a mass attack on the Muslims of the city. The truth of these claims continues to be highly debatable. Regardless of the truth, the popular belief was that the Muslims had caused the deaths and that the action called for revenge. A member of the BJP, when asked to comment on the situation, allegedly said, 'To every action there is an equal and opposite reaction.'

It is a matter of great concern that the Hindu rioters had been able to get access to the electoral registers to find out where the Muslim victims lived. At the same time reports suggest that the police did little to stop the attacks. However, the matter of greatest concern was the inactivity of the government. The then Prime Minister, A.B. Vajpayee, when asked to comment on the events reportedly remarked, 'Let us not forget how the whole thing started. Who lit the fire? Wherever in the world Muslims live, they tend not to live peacefully with others.' Such comments, regardless of who made them, are clear indicators of the mammoth efforts required to do away with communalism, especially since its flames are apparently being fanned by some from the very top.

The consequences of the riots were far reaching. It is estimated that some 200 000 were made homeless as a result of the riots. They were forced to go and live in refugee camps. However, the government did virtually nothing to help them. Most of the help that was provided came from the Islamiya Relief Committee, a charity run by hard-line Sunnis. It is therefore hardly surprising that many who went to these camps were radicalised, adding further to the problem of communalism.

Aid to Learning

1. What evidence is there that the government and police have done little to prevent communal unrest?
2. For each of the major incidents of unrest, decide what the major cause of the violence was. You should now be able to frame a report on the likely causes of communal violence.

Conclusion

There was, however, a backlash against this 'Hindu nationalism' as the election results of 2004 demonstrated. BJP's defeat in the elections indicated that the aggression had gone too far for most Indians. In Gujarat, following the violence of 2002, Muslim and Hindu business leaders took out adverts in the press and asked for calm by saying, 'Gujarat is and will continue to remain business friendly'. In other states, riots have been usually confined to a few volatile centres. Therefore, it is fairer to conclude that, outside of the vested

Fig. 3.19   School students on a rally to promote unity and harmony

interests of political leaders and sensationalism caused by the media, most Hindus and Muslims get on together reasonably well if left on their own.

Despite the episodes in communalism, it is not the dominant feature of the politics or the ideologies of the Indian people. Although political parties have often exploited it to gain power, most of those who voted for them were actually driven by economic and political concerns. The Indian people are still largely secular and the supporters of communalism are indeed a minority. In areas where there have been communal riots, the divide between Hindus and Muslims is not permanent.

Activities

- Find out about the organisations, both governmental and non-governmental, working towards achieving communal harmony in India. How successful have they been and what kind of activities are they engaged in? Make a presentation in your class.
- What can an average Indian citizen do in his/her every day life to promote communal harmony in India? Have a class discussion and prepare a list of action points.

Exercise

1. What are the reasons behind the apparent decline in communal violence?
2. Assess the reasons for communal violence in India.
3. How serious have the communal riots been in the period since 1984?
4. Assess the reasons for the growth and significance of communalism-based political parties in India.
5. How successful has government legislation been in dealing with communal violence?
6. Why has it proved to be so difficult to reduce communal violence in India?

Chapter 11

Affirmative Action

Why is affirmative action controversial? How effective has positive discrimination been?

Affirmative Action: Meaning

Affirmative action stands for the granting of special benefits to those from 'backward' communities. Backward communities can be defined as those from the so-called 'lower' castes and the Scheduled Tribes. This action may include reserving a certain percentage of job vacancies in an organisation for people from these communities or reserving a certain number of seats within the Parliament for them. The most notable cases have been the reservation of educational scholarships or posts in the public sector. However, to obtain the benefit one has to be classified as belonging to part of a backward community. The first step towards this came with the Mandal Report of 1980.

Controversy Around Affirmative Action

Much of the opposition to affirmative action is framed on the grounds of reverse discrimination and unwarranted preferences. The reservation of jobs or other benefits for certain groups means that certain others will be excluded. Those who traditionally held the higher posts will resent the potential threat to their position. This is particularly true in the case of education. A good education opens up the possibility of a good job and the chance to earn a high salary.

Higher educational opportunities had been traditionally dominated by members of the 'higher' castes. But with the opening up of opportunities for the 'lower' castes, it meant that their dominance in both education and employment was under threat. More people were now competing for the same job and some of the jobs were reserved to go to those from the 'lower' castes. Affirmative action, therefore, means that in practice the number of 'upper' castes who obtain the top jobs will be reduced.

Those who are opposed to affirmative action argue that it will lead to a kind of 'brain drain'. In their view, reserving seats at educational institutions will serve only to lower standards and bring down the morale of the students. This could then have an impact on the new technological industries, such as the IT industry, on which so much of India's recent progress is based. There are also not enough qualified candidates from the 'lower' castes who can eventually become professionals.

Fig. 3.20 Educational reservations led to mass protest

These problems can only be addressed by improving the standard of primary and secondary education. The shortage of colleges and vocational training institutions also means that there is a tough competition among the aspirants who are not part of any reservation for each and every available seat. At the same time, this also has an impact on India's economic development as certain industries absorb most of the well-qualified professionals, leaving very few for the other sectors. There are also concerns that investors will think twice before investing in India because of the lack of opportunities for the more able. The situation has been made more controversial by discussions on reserving half the jobs in the private sector for the 'lower' castes as this will have a massive impact on India's competitiveness.

Entrance requirements for universities are also seen as unfair. Applicants in the reserved category are required to score much less in competitive exams in comparison to those in the general category. Perhaps a bigger concern is that many of those from the reserved quota have difficulty in completing their courses because of the lack of language skills. Many of them went to village schools where they were taught in their local language, but at higher level urban schools they are taught in English. Some students had to be allowed to give their oral answers in their local language.

The desire of some to extend the privileges of affirmative action to other 'backward' caste groups has further added to the controversy. Suggestions that certain castes should be added to the list of those entitled to privileges have given rise to the problems. The demand is that, in addition to the existing 22 per cent of places reserved in colleges, a further 28 per cent would be added, making the total number of reserved places 50 per cent of all the available seats.

Aid to Learning

Much of the opposition to affirmative action has been over educational changes.
Why do you think that this area has been particularly controversial?

The Effect of Positive Discrimination

The reservation system has made a significant difference. It would be accurate to suggest that, thanks to reservation, India's two hundred million Dalits now interact on a much more regular basis with the rest of the Indian society. Dalits have also had increased opportunities to improve their economic and social position, so much so, that in 2002 a Dalit, Dr K.R. Narayanan, was elected president.

Fig. 3.21   Dr K.R. Narayanan

The electoral sphere is one area where the caste based quota system has been achieved. The reserved constituencies have resulted in a major change in the caste composition of elected representatives. These used to be dominated by members of the upper castes until the 1980s. The emergence of Dalit parties and their role in key offices will ensure that their issues remain at the front of politics.

The picture becomes more complex when an examination of employment and education is made. A study of Delhi University has shown that the quotas are only about half filled. It might be argued that if this is the situation in the capital city, it is likely to be even worse elsewhere in the country. In the non-teaching jobs a different picture emerges, particularly where menial work is concerned. The menial jobs are nearly always carried out by Dalits. It is interesting to note that there is never any complaint about over-representation of the 'lower' castes in these low-paid jobs.

An examination of government jobs suggests that at lower levels the quotas are nearly always filled. But at the higher levels the picture is less satisfactory. The figures are similar to those at Delhi University as a variety of procedures, both formal and informal, are used to keep the 'lower' castes out. This includes temporary positions, interviews, personality tests and adverse entries in personal files.

At the same time, there are many who now believe that the scheme has become an obstacle to further progress among India's poor. This is because the aim of the 'backward' caste parties has simply become the acquisition of more and more reserved places. If they fail to achieve this, they lose power.

It is argued that success depends upon delivering jobs. This was clearly seen in 2004 when Laloo Prasad Yadav provided Manmohan Singh with the votes that got him elected. His reward was the Ministry of Railways. This was a very powerful position as the workforce numbers 1.5 million people, and can obviously be used to provide a large number of jobs to the supporters. However, it also meant that the minister could now oppose any redeployment or rationalisation of the workforce that will lessen his influence. He also opposed all privatisation schemes and tried to get the reservation system extended to private industry so that his influence could increase further.

This is a clear evidence of the fact that the reservation system encourages the underprivileged to vote for those who will get them a job and not those who will improve their overall condition.

There has been more progress and success in the urban south, particularly in Tamil Nadu. This may be because the process of affirmative action and reserved jobs has been in place much longer. It started in Tamil Nadu in 1920 and now nearly 70 per cent of government jobs are reserved for the 'backward' castes. As a result, the 'upper' castes and the 'backward' castes have been working together much more closely for far longer than in the rest of India. Tamil Nadu is seen as the best state in terms of looking after 'backward' groups.

Activities

Complete the table given below

Issue	Evidence of Success	Evidence of Failure	Extent of Success
Education			
Jobs			
Social			
Electoral			
Regional			

Conclusion

To conclude, it can be argued that access to education and employment has been spread widely through affirmative action. But the distribution of this access has been uneven. The reservation programme has redeemed many from a state of subservience and humiliation and given them greater opportunities. However, those who have gained from affirmative action might find that they face social rejection. In the long run, education is likely to help remove the prejudiced association of Dalits with ignorance and incompetence.

But this is going to take time. Most importantly, it has kept the problems of those who have gained from the process at the forefront of the educated as there has not been any drive for their inclusion going beyond government policy. It can, therefore, be safely argued that affirmative action has been a partial success. It has accelerated the growth of a middle class and the 'backward' castes have been brought into roles that would have been unimaginable a few years ago.

Exercise

1. How serious are the problems faced by the 'lower' castes and scheduled tribes in India today?
2. Why has it proved difficult to solve the problems faced by the 'lower' castes and scheduled tribes?
3. 'Economic development is the most important reason why the difficulties faced by the 'lower' castes and scheduled tribes are being overcome.' How far do you agree?
4. Assess the reasons why education is such an important issue for the 'lower' castes and scheduled tribes.
5. Why has affirmative action caused so much controversy?
6. How successful have governments been since 1984 in dealing with the problems faced by the 'lower' castes and scheduled tribes?

Unit 4 India and the World

Aims of the Unit

- Understand what issues have affected India's foreign relations since 1989
- Evaluate the on-going conflicts with Pakistan
- Understand India's relations with Russia and China
- Evaluate the impact of the rise of Hindu nationalism on foreign relations
- Discuss India's relations with its regional neighbours
- Understand the change in relations with USA

Key Concepts

Cold War: The period between 1945 and 1991 when there was hostility between the West and the communist powers

Diplomacy: The way in which countries deal with other countries, discussing issues and making treaties and alliances

Globalisation: Free trade with other countries and the end of undue economic controls

Hindu Nationalism: Political and religious movements in India to promote the interests of the Hindu majority

Jihadism: The belief held by fundamentalist Muslims that they are fighting a 'holy war' against non-believers

Liberal Democracy: The belief in parliament and equal voting rights, with the individual's freedom being protected against the State

Non Alignment: India's policy (under Nehru's leadership) of not associating with the political ideology of either 'side' during the Cold War

Terrorism: The belief that political change can be brought about by acts of violence to destabilise regimes

'War on Terror': Campaign launched by US President George W. Bush against what he saw as international terrorist groups like Al Qaeda

Time Line

1990 – First Gulf War

1992 – India as 'dialogue partner' with ASEAN

1997 – India as member of BIMSTEC

1998 – India's Nuclear Test

1999 – Kargil War between India and Pakistan

2001 – India-Pakistan summit

2005 – Earthquake in Pakistan leading to more India-Pakistan cooperation

2008 – Mumbai terrorist attacks

2011 – India becomes a non-permanent member of the UN Security Council

Introduction

This unit deals with India's relations with other countries since 1989. The rapid growth of the Indian economy, the rise of Hindu nationalism and the ending of Congress' predominant position along with the development of nuclear power have all affected India's foreign relations. India has become more linked to Southeast Asia and has built up her regional, political and economic influence in a 'Look East' policy. This policy is a manifestation of India's focused foreign policy orientation towards an immensely resourceful and flourishing region.

It has continued to prove difficult to resolve the disputes with Pakistan as the rise of Islamic extremism became a new factor. India's desire to be a nuclear power also led to disputes with the United States. Since 2001, however, there have been changes as the US has become closer to India. There have hence been more attempts to end the Kashmir dispute. India has also developed its military capacity and its trade and other links with the ASEAN countries. India is seen more and more as a superpower in the making.

Fig. 4.1   Manmohan Singh at the ASEAN summit in 2011

The issue is whether India has the will and the resources to take on the wider regional and world responsibilities that the superpower status demands.

On 1 January 2011, India became a non-permanent member of the UN Security Council with the approval of other superpowers. India's rising international importance as opposed to mere regional importance was demonstrated by this development. The Chinese Premier, Wen Jiabao, who came on a visit to New Delhi in December 2010 said:

> China understands and supports India's aspiration to play a greater role in the United Nations including in the Security Council.

India has come a long way since 1947 and is now a major economic, military and diplomatic influence on the world stage.

Aid to Learning

1. Why do you think India's desire to be a nuclear power led to disputes with the United States?
2. What do you understand by the term 'superpower'? Which nations of the world qualify to be called superpowers today?
3. From what you have read in unit 2 and unit 3, discuss what could be the potential obstacles to India's becoming a superpower.

Chapter 12 Changing Relationships

Key Question

What do India's relations with the neighbouring states of South and Southeast Asia reveal about India's needs and interests as a regional superpower?

This chapter deals with the 'redefining' of India's role as it moved from the post-colonial to its superpower status. It will also explore the major changes seen at the start of the twenty-first century. As India grew economically in the 1990s, it developed greater links in the region. Indian emigration spread its influence; the end of the Cold War and the rise of Islamic militancy also changed the traditional context of Indian policy.

Economic Growth

A fundamental change took place in India's policy of economic modernisation during the 1990s. The Indian government abandoned the Nehru model of a socialist-style economy with central planning and high tariffs (import duties) based on heavy industry. Previous policies proved inadequate to cope with the serious domestic and international problems facing India. The new Indian economy needed economic links with other countries, greater trade with Southeast Asia, agreements about power supplies and more diverse markets. It no longer looked up to Soviet-style models of planned economic growth. Instead, it started subscribing to the western capitalist models of free market economy. Corresponding to the change in economic policy, the foreign policy changed as well. After the dissolution of the Soviet Union, India improved its relations with the United States, Canada, France, Japan and Germany.

Activities

Why is economic strength or weakness such an important element in foreign policy? Discuss in class.

Indian Diaspora

One of the major changes in the post-Nehru period was the emergence of the so-called Indian diaspora. Millions of Indians had started working and living abroad making India a part of the international scene in a new way. Foreign influences could be seen in the growth of the IT industry, in the change in Indian cities, in its technology and culture. Similarly, Indian influences could also be noticed in other countries as well. Indian foreign policy started establishing new relationships with other countries and groups of countries.

The official figures (May 2012) for Indians working or living abroad come to an astonishing 21.9 million. Initially, in the post-1947 period, emigrants were unskilled, but the 'new diaspora' includes many skilled workers, especially in the US and the Middle East. 205 countries have Indians living or working in them. Australia has 448 000, while Singapore has 670 000. The UK has over 1.5 million. This is one of the largest movements of people in modern times.

The Indian diaspora thus constitutes a diverse, heterogeneous and eclectic global community representing different regions, languages, cultures and faiths. They are today amongst the best educated and successful communities in the world.

The End of the Cold War

Another major change was the end of the Cold War in 1991. The old orientation towards the Soviet Union was no longer a way for India to protect itself against China or to get the necessary technology to deal with any conflict with Pakistan. There had to be new alignments. India also had to build up her defences. In 1989, India took a major decision by holding underground nuclear tests and accelerating its nuclear programme in defiance of international opinion.

Focus

The Cold War

During World War II, Britain and USA joined hands with Russia against Hitler. But after the war, conflicts arose over Eastern Europe. There was no direct combat between Russia and the US but a long period of hostility called the Cold War ensued. Both sides had atomic weapons. Hence, had it come to actual, physical combat, the consequences would have been dire. As both the sides wanted to have their influence over the whole world, countries like India were affected by the Cold War. The Cold War ended in 1991 with the disintegration of USSR.

The Growth of Islamic Radicalism

Another major challenge was the growth of radical Islamic movements. The West had supported the resistance against Russia in Afghanistan when Russian forces had entered the country in 1979. This, while changing relationships in the long run, helped to develop a new religious radicalism which came to resent American domination. The Gulf War in 1990–1991 against Iraq was seen as an attempt by the US to gain domination over the Middle East.

Western culture was seen by a new generation of Islamic radicals as undermining traditional values. The resentment and anger came to a head with the attacks on the World Trade Centre on 11 September, 2001. This created new problems for India and changed the nature of the Kashmir issue. Now the conflict over Kashmir became a part of a wider struggle between Islamic fundamentalists and their enemies. India had to be more aware of the Islamic terrorism that has made such an impact on the western world.

Focus

The Gulf War

The Gulf War (1991) was fought by an alliance led by the US to support Kuwait, a Western ally, when the Iraqi army, commanded by the ruler Saddam Hussein, invaded Kuwait. The main battles were aerial and ground combat within Iraq, Kuwait and the bordering areas of Saudi Arabia. The war did not expand outside of the immediate border region, although Iraq fired missiles on Israeli cities. The easy victory of the western forces created concerns in the Arab world, which already disliked the US support for Israel in the Middle East and its influence in Pakistan.

New Relations with the US

In the post-Independence period, relations between the US and India were strained. India seemed to be more aligned with the USSR. Therefore, US diplomacy tended to favour Pakistan, India's rival. Personal relations between US leaders and those of India were often cold.

After 9/11, India extended strong support to the US and there was a diplomatic revolution. The US, despite having mistrusted India earlier, decided to change relations between them radically. President Bush supported the Indian nuclear defence programme. India and the US grew far closer than in the days of the Cold War as seen from the positive progress in bilateral relations on the nuclear issue, sanctions, and defence cooperation.

9/11

'9/11' refers to the events of September 2001 when members of the Islamic terrorist organisation, Al Qaeda, hijacked four internal US planes. These planes were flown into the World Trade Centre, New York and the Pentagon. It was an immensely shocking and extremely disastrous event because of which George W. Bush, the then President, declared a 'War on Terror' which involved US troops invading Iraq and Afghanistan.

The Saudi terrorist leader Osama Bin Laden was not found until 2011 when he was killed by the US forces who had discovered his hiding place in Pakistan.

Fig. 4.2 The twin towers of World Trade Centre during the attack on 11 September 2001

Israel

After decades of non-aligned and pro-Arab policy, India formally established relations with Israel in January 1992 and ties between the two nations have flourished since, primarily due to common strategic interests and security threats. An important development was greater diplomatic and economic contacts, with Israel supplying vital defence equipment for India. India is the largest customer of Israeli military equipment and Israel is the second-largest military partner of India.

Israel

Like India, Israel gained independence from Britain after World War II (in May 1948). Similar to India, there were territorial struggles and religious divisions in the new country involving the Jews and the Muslim Arabs.

However, Israel's situation was very different from India's with the Jews being the minority. India was sympathetic to the Palestinians and to the enemies of Israel. It did not wish to alienate its 160 million Muslim citizens or its Muslim neighbours by establishing relations with Israel. This was also followed because of the policy of the USSR with whom India was friendly. This policy, however, was changed after 1989.

Pakistan

The long standing disputes between India and Pakistan have not disappeared and there was a major military conflict with Pakistan over Kashmir in 1991. However, there were pressures for negotiation and serious talks were resumed in 2004. The increased economic links with Pakistan made it sensible to try and resolve political differences. Despite terrorism by Islamic militants, India has been restrained in its responses. It is worthy of note that the Mumbai attacks of November 2008 did not lead to an armed conflict with Pakistan. India made a distinction between the responsibility of elements in Pakistan and the government of Pakistan, which was quick to condemn the violence.

China and Southeast Asia

Similarly with China, disputes still exist. But India has done its best to improve its trade links with China which now stand at the highest since 1949, though not necessarily huge in terms of actual volume. India has worked to improve its economic relations with Southeast Asia as well. There is much less idealistic talk about improving the state of the under-developed world and the responsibility of the developed countries in that mission. Instead, there is a lot more practical economic cooperation since 1989 than in the period before. Both nations have realised the need for cooperation and for moving away from old animosities through mutual agreements. They have resolved to find solutions to their disputes through negotiations.

Focus

China

The communist regime in China, based on peasant support, was led by Mao Zedong. This brought the Cold War to Asia. Since 1949, China has emerged as a very strong military and economic power.

Initially, the Indian leaders saw China as another post-colonial Asian power and sought its friendship. However, cooperation with China proved difficult because of border issues and the war of 1962 was a blow to Nehru's beliefs in post-colonial nations working together. The border issues have never been resolved.

Fig. 4.3   Mao Zedong (1949) declaring the founding of People's Republic of China

Aid to Learning

1. What do you understand by Cold War and how has it affected India?
2. In what ways has Islamic radicalism been a problem for India?
3. What have been the two most important changes in Indian policy since 1989?

   (Hint: You are going to learn more about this in the rest of the unit. For the while, just make a first judgement, explain it and then return to it later to see if you still think the same. You can always change your mind.)

The Current Situation

The period since 1989 has seen a major reorientation of Indian foreign policy. It has also seen strong elements of continuity because of the problems of territorial disputes inherited from the British Raj. Indian foreign policy is not a luxury for India's leaders, but a vital necessity.

- The problems with China, a large and powerful neighbour, are potentially very dangerous. Its aggressive foreign policy postures do not encourage a benign view of it. Many in India reckon China to be the major future threat to India.
- The problems with Pakistan have been made worse by the increasing internal problems of Pakistan and the existence of radical Islamic groups in Pakistan's border provinces eager to resist the Western-supported regime in Afghanistan. These groups are also a threat to India which lost 2 500 lives in incidents of internal unrest in 2008.
- The problems of Bangladesh too have their impact on India through the refugees who come into India to escape extreme poverty and natural disasters caused by climate change.
- Economic growth requires India to develop economic links with other Asian countries which in turn gave rise to ethical problems, for example, the issue of dealing with the repressive military regime in Burma. 'The re-emergence of a more democratic Burma offers opportunities for India to support change by economic cooperation.'
- As Indian economic growth makes it a major power, it is expected to take a distinct position on major world issues. It is likewise expected to play its part in international actions to deal with global issues such as recession, climate change, ecological protection and human rights. India has had an impressive growth and has some world class institutions, but several other indicators are unfortunately poor.

Activities

- 'Growth, for a nation, is always a relative term.' Have a class debate on this with special attention to the case of India.
- Discuss why it is essential for India to be involved in global issues such as recession, climate change, ecological protection and human rights.

Exercise

1. Why has it been difficult for India to improve relations with Pakistan?
2. What impact has the rise of Islamic fundamentalism had on India's foreign relations?
3. Why have relations between India and China not been uniformly good?
4. Why have relations between India and the US improved?
5. What impact has the end of the Cold War had on India's foreign relations?
6. What expectations are there about the world role of India now that were not present before c. 1990?

Chapter 13 — India's Relation with Pakistan

Key Question

Why does India have on-going problems with Pakistan?

Territorial Dispute

The arrangement made when India and Pakistan were created as separate countries in 1947 was that the 560-odd princely states who owed allegiance to Britain should decide which of the new countries to join. The Maharaja of Jammu and Kashmir, a state formed by the British after the Sikh War of 1846 and including diverse territories, ruled over Buddhists, Hindus and Muslims. There was, however, a Muslim majority in Kashmir, the largest part of the state.

The Maharaja of Jammu and Kashmir agreed to sign the Instrument of Accession (October, 1947) with India due to an armed intrusion by local tribesmen from across the border aided by the Pakistani armed forces. In the combat that ensued, Indian forces established control over about two-thirds of the territory, before a United Nations ceasefire in January 1949 was announced. Both sides agreed to a referendum to ask the people what they wanted, but this has never happened. The essential points of the difference in opinion between India and Pakistan can be summarised as following.

- India believed that Jammu and Kashmir was no different from any other princely state and that the ruler, having signed the Instrument of Accession, had decided for India. So, legally, that gave India the right to the territory because the Maharaja alone had the right and power to take a decision for his state. Legal and constitutional rights were important benchmarks for the new India.
- According to Pakistan, India had pressurised the Maharaja and that natural justice demanded that a largely Muslim area be given the right to decide if it wanted to join Pakistan. For Pakistan, these were not just insignificant border areas. The name Pakistan itself, as coined in 1933, refers to its different constituent groups, namely Punjabis, Afghans and, most importantly, Kashmiris. So, Kashmir was considered an integral part of the new State from the coining of the name Pakistan itself in 1933.

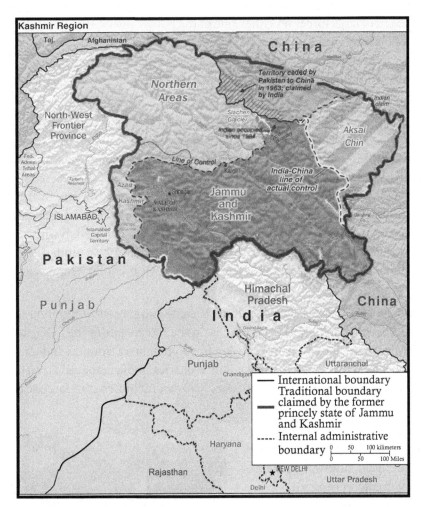

Map 4.1   Kashmir region

Aid to Learning

Explain why there was such a dispute between India and Pakistan over Jammu and Kashmir.

(Hint: Put the reasons on cards and then try putting them in order of importance. Remember, 'explain why' is not the same as 'describe what happened'.)

The Situation by 1989

A border dispute, which was initially part of a complex process of establishing two new independent States in 1947, had escalated by 1989 to become a symbol of national pride for both countries.

The deployment of large forces on either side of the border meant that the military reputation of both countries was at stake. By 1989, a further complication had emerged with the growth of radical Islamic groups in the backwash from the struggle between Islamic fighters in Afghanistan, the overthrow of the Shah of Iran and the establishment of an Islamist regime.

In 1989, a widespread popular and armed Islamic insurgency started in Kashmir. These insurgents were discontented about the failure to get representation in the 1987 state legislative assembly election. They were divided in their aims, some wanting union with Pakistan and others independence for Kashmir. Pakistan demanded a referendum which India refused, now categorising the problem as one of internal terrorism. By this time, both countries had taken determined steps towards armament, creating further distrust. India had begun to develop its atomic capacity since 1974 as opposed to which Pakistan developed surface to surface missiles assisted by China in the 1990s. Both sides conducted underground nuclear tests in 1998. The potential for nuclear conflict, however, did not deter conventional conflict.

Armed conflict broke out in 1999 when India became aware of the infiltration of Pakistani soldiers and Kashmiri militants into positions on the Indian side of the LOC, north of Kargil. Pakistan claimed that the troops were freedom fighters from the Indian side of Kashmir while India saw them as Pakistani mercenaries. India launched air strikes and artillery bombardments against the intrusion. Pakistan mobilised on a large scale and huge forces were assembled.

On both sides of the Line of Control, there were substantial refugees from the war. Once again, disproportionate military mobilisation produced only a standoff and put back the possibility of achieving a long term solution. Domestically, the electorates of both countries were unwilling to compromise. The considerable rise in the feeling of Hindu nationalism also made any concession difficult. In Pakistan, the surrender of claims was likely to fuel the militant Islamic groups and lead to destabilisation.

Fig. 4.4 The Kargil War Memorial

Yet, in terms of India's position, some other solution than long-term hostility with occasional eruptions of costly warfare in remote mountains was required. India's growing economy was built on greater global trade and investment. Investors were not likely to be impressed by border wars. India was already cut off from much of the world opinion by its 1998 nuclear tests.

It was condemned by the Security Council of the UN and its fellow members of the G8 summit of rich countries. United States continued to favour Pakistan since it was important as a Muslim ally and an aid in suppressing militancy.

From 1999, India started receiving vital US diplomatic help as the US became unusually sympathetic to India due to the Kargil War. Efforts were made to pursue talks with Pakistan to avoid a clash of interests since the US was supporting Pakistan as well as improving its relations with India.

The Summit of 2001

In the summer of 2001, the Agra summit was held between Pakistani President Pervez Musharraf and Indian Prime Minister Atal Bihari Vajpayee. It was organised with the aim of resolving long-standing issues between India and Pakistan. The summit started amid high hopes of resolving various disputes between the two countries but no formal agreement could be attained as both sides remained inflexible. Pakistan was eager to end the Simla Agreement of 1972 which had established the status quo of Kashmir borders. But to India the problem remained that Pakistan was supporting 'rebel' movements in Kashmir.

Fig. 4.5 Pervez Musharraf and A.B. Vajpayee at the Agra Summit

On-going Conflict

In October 2001, there was a devastating attack on the Kashmiri assembly in Srinagar, the capital of Jammu and Kashmir, in which 38 people were killed. After the attack, the Chief Minister of Indian-administered Kashmir, Farooq Abdullah, called on the Indian Government to launch a war against the militant training camps across the border in Pakistan.

On 13 December, an armed attack on the Indian Parliament in New Delhi left 14 people dead. India accused terrorists backed by Pakistan and also supplied proofs to the Pakistani Government against Jaish-i-Mohammed and Lashkar-e-Toiba. The attack led to a dramatic build-up of troops along the Indo-Pakistan border, military exchanges and heightened fears of a more intense conflict.

Negotiations and Violence

In January 2002, President Musharraf gave a keynote speech pledging that Pakistan would not allow terrorists to operate from Pakistani soil. He called on the Government of India to resolve the dispute over Jammu and Kashmir through dialogue. However, relations between India and Pakistan continued to be troubled. Terrorism within Indian Kashmir brought another war scare in summer 2002, but by April 2003 India and Pakistan were talking about restoring air links, diplomatic ties and even cricket test matches.

It was difficult to go into the more fundamental matters concerning a long-term solution when violent incidents and a volatile public opinion were making even normal diplomatic communications difficult. The long-running religious conflict over the Babri Masjid in India and the violent attacks on Muslims in Gujarat in 2002 made it difficult for good-will to be generated.

Earthquake Diplomacy 2005

In 2005, a natural disaster facilitated more harmonious relations. On 8 October 2005, a major earthquake killed more than 70 000 people in Pakistan including some in Pakistan-controlled Kashmir. The disaster affected India and Indian Kashmir as well. Therefore, India offered assistance to Pakistan. Practicalities required relaxation of the restrictions on border crossing with telephone lines being restored and the opening of crossings for relief convoys. In a parallel to the Berlin Wall, families were allowed to cross the line of control in November 2005. This sense of co-operation brought more hopes for a settlement. However, at the same time, there was continuing escalation of terrorism with bomb attacks in New Delhi on 29 October and Karachi on 15 November, respectively.

Fig. 4.6　Damage caused by the 2005 Pakistan Earthquake

The violence was not entirely by activists supporting Indian or Pakistani control. They were Kashmiri nationalists and criminal elements seeking to disrupt a permanent solution. International and economic pressures were at work for a settlement. India and Pakistan had agreed to troop-withdrawals from Kashmir's Siachen Glacier and to transport links between Indian and Pakistani territories.

India's Relations with Afghanistan

India has had a long history of ties with Afghanistan. But these had come to be disrupted in the light of the rise of Taliban in the 1990s. India did not approve of this militant regime and was hopeful when the US-led invasion put an end to it. In fact, India aided the overthrow of the Taliban and became the largest regional provider of humanitarian and reconstruction-related aid to Afghanistan. India gave and continues to give substantial aid to the new regime there. Between 2001 and 2008, this amounted to $750m and in 2008 another $450m was agreed upon. India had a number of considerations in this regard. The most important of them are listed below.

- Ensuring that Afghanistan did not align itself with Pakistan
- Afghanistan as a gateway to the energy supplies with the Central Asian countries such as Turkmenistan, Kazakhstan and Tajikistan
- Promoting stability in the border region
- Aligning itself to the US policy.

India has helped Tajikistan modernise hydroelectricity and has also signed a deal for a natural gas pipeline from Turkmenistan through Afghanistan to India. To protect the 4000 Indian workers in Afghanistan, India has also sent 500 special paramilitary police.

India has helped with the construction projects and given support in matters of health, education and transport to President Karzai. Trade between these two countries is increasing and India has invested in the Iranian port of Chabahar to provide a link with Afghanistan while avoiding passage through Pakistan. India's approach has largely been a function of the desire to prevent Pakistan from dominating that country, and maintaining overall regional balance.

Aid to Learning

1. What was India's attitude towards the Taliban regime in Afghanistan?
2. Why is it important for India to support and maintain good relations with Afghanistan?
3. In which particular aspects has India been especially supportive of Afghanistan? Why do you think it is so?

Activities

As a foreign policy expert, draw up a short briefing document for the Indian Government on the importance of Afghanistan for India.

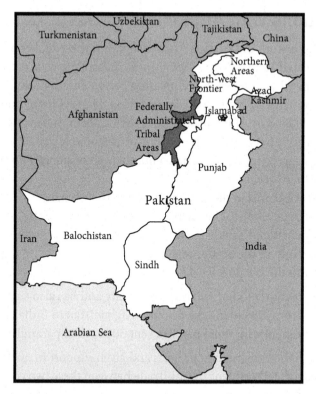

Map 4.2　Pakistan and neighbouring countries

Pakistan, on the other hand, saw Afghanistan as a natural sphere of influence and extended its support to the Taliban. It objected to India's opening of four consulates and feared encirclement if a pro-Indian regime got established in Afghanistan. An Indian air base in Farkor in Tajikistan alarmed the Pakistani defence planners even more. There have also been accusations that India has been encouraging separatism in the Pakistani province of Baluchistan. India is also said to be threatening Pakistan's trade with Afghanistan and its own outlet at Gwadar, built with China's help.

The Situation by 2009

There are other additional conflicts which have not helped in gaining a comprehensive settlement over disputed territory. There have been both 'plus' and 'minus' factors for peace. The 'plus' factors include the need for greater trade, cooperation over energy projects, the need to stabilise the region by controlling Islamic militancy and to work with the United States. The 'minus' factors include the impact of terrorism, China's support for Pakistan, Pakistan's fears of encirclement and the long history of war and conflict.

Terrorism has proved to be an on-going and increasingly disturbing problem. However, by 2008, there were signs that terrorist outrages might not succeed in holding back further negotiations. By 2009, Pakistan was clearly taking action against its Taliban supporters.

They have accepted India's view that Pakistan should not be used as a base for terrorism against India. Peace talks began anew at Sharm-el-Sheikh in July.

There was speculation that both sides wanted to gain US approval and the talks were under way before a visit by Hillary Clinton, the new US Secretary of State in the Obama administration. The topics of discussion were Indian presence in Afghanistan, which Pakistan resented, as well as concerns about Islamic terrorism operating from Pakistan. Once again, other issues pushed Kashmir aside.

Fig. 4.7   Pakistani Prime Minister Yousaf Raza Gillani and Indian Prime Minister Dr Manmohan Singh at Sharm el-Sheikh, a conference centre in Egypt

Exercise

1. Explain how each of the following has affected relations between India and Pakistan.
    (a) Jammu and Kashmir since 1989
    (b) Indian influence in Afghanistan
    (c) Terrorism
    (d) Energy supplies
    (e) Economic cooperation in the region
2. Write a report with maps explaining (a) the state of the relationship between India and Afghanistan, and (b) why India sees Afghanistan as important.
3. Discuss in class the situation in Kashmir:
    (a) Why has this old problem not been resolved yet?
    (b) How could it be resolved to the benefit of all involved:
        • India gives up some or all of its claims?
        • Pakistan gives up some or all its claims?
        • Let the people of Jammu and Kashmir and Ladakh decide for themselves?
        • Give it a large degree of autonomy?
        • Make it an independent country?

Chapter 14   India and Global Politics

Key Question

To what extent has India's foreign policy changed as a result of the end of the Cold War?

The 'Look East' Policy

Before 1991, India's foreign policy was not strongly focused on Southeast Asia. It was dominated by concerns about Pakistan, China and its relations with the USSR together with a general concern over international influence by maintaining official 'non-alignment' and appealing for more support for the Third World. After 1991, with greater economic liberalisation and globalisation, India turned towards establishing greater relations with other countries in the region and increasing its economic and political status as an Asian power.

India's 'Look East' policy was developed and enacted during the governments of Narsimha Rao (1991–1996) and Atal Bihari Vajpayee (1998–2004). India developed economic links, greater strategic cooperation and cultural ties with Southeast Asia. In this, it emerged as a rival of China in terms of influence. This has been a major post-Cold War development.

Myanmar

As the world's largest democracy and in line with ethical standards in foreign policy, India had not had close links with the military dictatorship in Myanmar (Burma). After 1993, however, India changed course and put its material interests first. India's move to forge close relations was motivated by a desire to counter China's growing influence as a regional leader and enhance its own influence and standing. Following are the major consequences of this change.

- Trade and investment increased
- Indian firms built roads, ports and pipelines across borders
- Agreements were made with Myanmar about supplying natural gas and oil
- India helped to train Myanmar's armed forces and cooperated in suppressing separatism and drug trafficking in border areas.

This has brought India into potential conflict with China, who had been supplying Myanmar's armed forces and taking a lot of its natural gas. China's military presence along its coast and in the Coco Islands has led to greater Indian military build-up.

Economic and Military Cooperation

There have been trade treaties and military discussions between India and Singapore, Vietnam, Cambodia and the Philippines. India has increased trade and military co-operation with Sri Lanka and Thailand as well. Discussions with Taiwan, Japan and South Korea have also taken place for political cooperation and common strategic interest. Japan and South Korea have invested heavily in India.

Military agreements with Indonesia, Vietnam and Singapore have been accompanied by the development of India's Far East Naval Command based on the Andaman Islands off Port Blair. This was with the view to protecting the trade routes through the Malacca Straits.

India and International Organisations

Mekong Ganga Cooperation: This association of India, Thailand, Burma, Cambodia, Laos and Vietnam has led to ministerial meetings and working groups on four major areas, namely tourism, culture, education and transport.

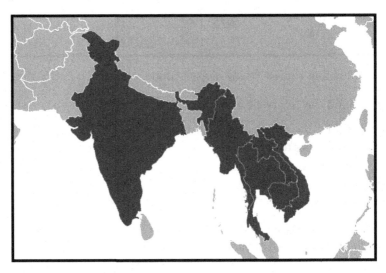

Map 4.3   Mekong Ganga Cooperation

Bay of Bengal Initiative for Multi-Sectoral Technical and Economic Cooperation (BIMSTEC): This originated in 1997 and India is its current chair. Its focus is on economic and technical development and on increasing trade. BIMSTEC provides a unique link between South Asia and Southeast Asia bringing together 1.3 billion people, a combined GDP of US$750 billion, and a considerable amount of complementarities.

Southeast Asian Association for Regional Co-operation (ASEAN): This important association accepted India as a 'dialogue partner' in 1992. Since then links between the member states have strengthened. India became a member of the Council for Security Cooperation in the Asia Pacific and a member of the ASEAN regional forum in 1996 and a summit level partner in 2002. India signed the Treaty of Amity and Co-operation in Southeast Asia in 2003. India has been seen by Japan and the US as a counter-weight to China's influence. India has worked on improved communication links in Southeast Asia.

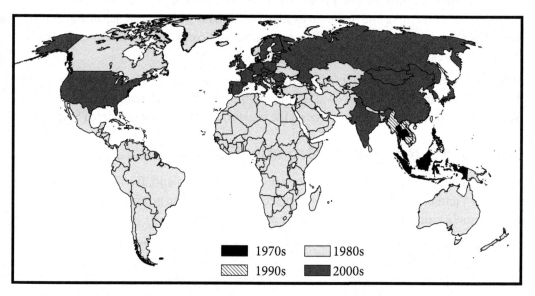

| ■ | 1970s | ▢ | 1980s |
| ▨ | 1990s | ■ | 2000s |

Map 4.4   Countries that signed Treaty of Amity and Cooperation in Southeast Asia

The principles behind the Treaty are as follows.

- Mutual respect for the independence of all nations
- The right of each state to be free from external interference
- Settlement of disputes by peaceful means
- Renunciation of the use of force
- Effective cooperation.

The 'ASEAN way' is to create durability and longevity within the organisation, by promoting regional identity and enhancing a spirit of mutual confidence and cooperation. ASEAN agreements are negotiated in a close, interpersonal process with consultations and consensus designed to engender a democratic approach to decision making. The potential for clashes with China remains considerable and Indian diplomacy has worked hard to maintain good economic and political relations. However, the appeal for India as an associate among the nations of Southeast Asia and for America is a counter-balance to Chinese ambitions.

In the past, India's engagement with much of Asia, including Southeast and East Asia, was built on an idealistic conception of Asian brotherhood, based on shared experiences of colonialism and of cultural ties. The rhythm of the region today is determined, however, as much by trade, investment and production as by history and culture. That is what motivates our decade-old Look East Policy. Already, this region accounts for 45 per cent of our external trade.

Yashwant Sinha,
Former External Affairs Minister
in a speech at Harvard University, 2003

Some economic effects of India's Look East policies are

- Korean companies have invested heavily in India, including a major steel works at Odisha
- Singapore has invested in chemical and IT industries
- Japan invested $33b in major road building between Delhi and Mumbai which began in 2008.

Strategic cooperation in Southeast Asia has led to

- Joint naval exercises with Singapore since 1993 and Vietnam since 2000
- Joint naval patrols in the Andaman Sea with Indonesia since 2002
- Joint military exercises with China in counter-terrorism
- Joint naval exercises with China in the East China Sea since 2003
- India's good relations with US allies — Australia, Singapore, Japan — have led to US military aid — the 2005 'New Framework for US-India Defence Relationship' was a significant step in promoting new defence agreements
- In April 2006, Australia, Japan, the US and India held joint naval exercises off the coast of Japan.

Energy as a Motive for Cooperation

India has to import considerable amounts of oil and gas. Other Asian countries are high users and high importers of the same. So, there has been a need for joint action to protect supplies, develop reserves and areas of energy supplies and also to conserve energy. In 2004, India took the initiative in a round table conference with China, Japan and South Korea for cooperation on oil and gas and starting a dialogue with the major oil-producers.

The combination of rising oil consumption and relatively flat production has left India increasingly dependent on imports to meet its petroleum demand. In 2010, India was the world's fifth largest net importer of oil, importing about 70 per cent of the total oil consumption. A majority of India's crude oil imports come from the Middle East, with Saudi Arabia and Iran supplying the largest shares. The share of Iranian oil in Indian imports has decreased in recent years, largely due to issues with processing payments.

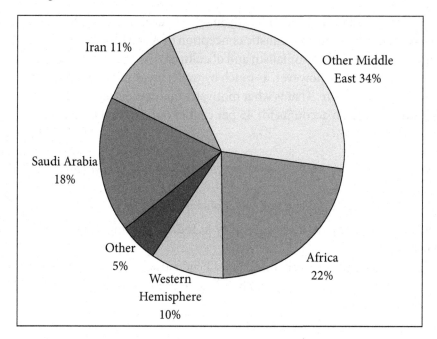

Fig. 4.8   India's oil imports by source, 2010

Though the government has taken steps in recent years to deregulate the hydrocarbons industry and encourage greater foreign involvement, state-owned enterprises predominate in India's oil sector. The largest player is state-owned Oil and Natural Gas Corporation (ONGC), which accounted for about three-quarters of India's oil production in 2009–2010.

Aid to Learning

Assess the importance of energy as motive for cooperation between India and its neighbours. Is it more important than military or diplomatic factors?

Peaceful Atomic Energy Cooperation Act

In the world of international conferences, meetings of ministers and optimistic reports and communiqués, what has emerged is India's potential as a major player in Asia. India has the potential for greater economic activity, a rational energy policy, strategic cooperation and greater security against terrorism.

However, in reality, the policy is a long-term shift and it is too early to make serious judgements. Commentators have pointed out its limitations. They are as follows.

- Some of the trade and investment has not been as much as expected. Japan's investment in and trade with India has been much less than that with China.

India's trade with Taiwan, in spite of all discussions, remained at under one per cent of Taiwan's total trade. Investments in China far outweigh investments in India. China's trade with Southeast Asia in 2006 was $160 billion while India's was substantially less than China's. India's imports from China have continued to outweigh China's imports from India.

- Increased economic activity and cooperation have not solved India's boundary disputes. The issues concerning Jammu and Kashmir remain unresolved as do the disputes with China over other areas. Insecurities demand a high level of military spending and preparation.
- In the major issue of North Korea — perhaps the greatest threat to peace in Asia — India has not played a leading role, even though it is deeply involved. This is because of the nuclear cooperation between Pakistan and North Korea, with Pakistan assisting North Korea's nuclear development in return for procuring missiles from the latter.
- In another major issue, namely, Taiwan, India has again not been a major participant, despite its close relations with both China and Taiwan. Given India's leading role in negotiating an end to the Korean War in 1950, it might be possible to see a decline in its real influence in spite of the high-sounding international pacts.
- The supply of arms, particularly light military helicopters to the dictatorial regime in Myanmar (Burma), has not helped India's reputation. It has been in contradiction to some of the more high-flown and idealistic aims of the international pacts. The military Junta continues to favour supplying China despite India's investment in gas supplies.

Aid to Learning

- How have India's relations with the wider world changed?
- What is the importance of energy for India?
- In groups decide what are the arguments (a) against India's developing its military power and being more assertive, and (b) what are the arguments that this is the right policy for India.

India's Relations with China

India's relations with China have been deeply influenced by the disappointment and shock of the war of 1962. China's new communist government came into power in 1949, following closely on India's Independence in 1947. The Communist victory was a break from foreign domination, just as the Indian Independence and the formation of Pakistan had been.

Nehru saw China as another Asian power that had broken free and hoped for good relations with it. Both countries pursued economic progress through state planning and both had large populations with strong regional differences. However, both had equally strong feelings of nationalism. Nehru accepted China's occupation of the neighbouring Tibet and tried to play down territorial clashes.

The Disputed Regions

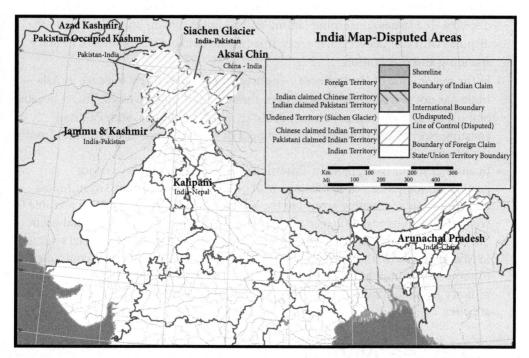

Map 4.5 Disputed areas

The key areas of contention with China were Aksai Chin on the Northeast frontier of Jammu and Kashmir and the northern frontier of Arunachal Pradesh in the Northeast. The northern border of the Indian state of Arunachal Pradesh follows a line drawn up in 1914. As the original agreement was between Britain and Tibet, China has never formally agreed to it and has claimed the northern part of the state. China also particularly resents being deprived of Tawang, which, though south of the McMahon Line, was occupied by Indian troops only in 1951. Aksai Chin is administered by China as part of its Xinjiang region but claimed by India as part of Jammu and Kashmir. In 1962, there was serious hostility over both this and Arunachal Pradesh but agreements in the 1990s established a Line of Actual Control as a temporary boundary.

Changes in China after 1976

After the death of Mao Zedong in 1976, China underwent massive economic change which made it a much stronger economic power than India. When India also began to change its economy after 1991, there were good reasons to rethink its hostile relations with China.

However, China continued to see India as a hostile power and was concerned about its nuclear potential. China was critical of the nuclear tests India held in 1989 and countered the threat by supplying military equipment and missiles to Pakistan. So, even after the fall of Communism in Russia, hostility between India and China continued.

Developments after 1989

Following Rajiv Gandhi's 1987 visit, there were arrangements for joint discussions on economic and scientific cooperation and annual ministerial meetings. China's Prime Minister, Li Eng, visited New Delhi in 1991 and in 1992, while President Venkataraman went to China. Negotiations took place from 1988 to 1993 and border trade was recommenced in 1992. Normal diplomatic relations were re-established. Formal border agreements were signed in 1993. Further talks in 1994 discussed trade and defence. In 1995, there were some troop withdrawals and more trade agreements.

India's Nuclear Tests

Nuclear tests conducted by India in 1998 put a brake on better relations, which had anyway been stained by a number of factors. These factors are as follows.

- China's supplying missiles to Pakistan
- China's increased influence in Myanmar, perceived as threat by India
- China's putting radar technicians on the Burmese Coco Islands
- The Tibetan exile groups agitating for independence from China.

However, unlike in the previous decades, when hostility dominated, India was more flexible given its need for more trade and in the context of a general 'Look East Policy'. It could not also rely on Russia for support any more. India had to try to neutralise China's support for Pakistan and to be able to focus its defence concerns on the problems arising from militant Islamic threats.

In 2000, the Indian President visited Beijing and the Chinese counterpart returned the visit in 2002. In 2003, Prime Minister Vajpayee went to China and negotiated the opening of two vital passes in the disputed region of Sikkim. Trade increased and there were greater economic ties. In 2006, there were agreements about a joint energy strategy. It was at this time that the Nathula pass through the Himalayas at Nathula was re-opened.

As with Pakistan, border disputes have continued to flare up from time to time. That said, high level visits and discussions on trade and some military cooperation have also continued. In 2008, India sent aid to the victims of China's Sichuan earthquake.

Evaluation: Outstanding Issues

- The official position in India is that China is occupying 14 000 sq. miles of territory in Northern Jammu and Kashmir. China still maintains its claim to 34 000 sq. miles of Arunachal Pradesh.
- There are about 100 000 Tibetan refugees in India, which China considers a threat, particularly with on-going anti-Chinese disturbances in Tibet. The Dalai Lama is also based in India. India restricts Tibetan political activities but this has been criticised by the opposition groups. China cannot be sure that Indian governments will always respect China's wishes.
- There has been much talk of a solution to the border issues and similar such changes. But India has been alarmed by China's demands for Tawang, a pilgrimage site for Tibetans in Arunachal Pradesh, and also by China's increasing road, rail and air links in the region. India has also increased its military presence in its new State and announced plans for a new road from Tawang to Mahadeopur. These moves do not indicate any desire for major concessions.
- A key development of 2008 which gave India access to non-military nuclear technology supported by the US in the NSG was opposed by China.
- China fears closer defence links between India and the US. These include the sale of the Hercules military transport aircraft and helicopters and the granting of access to the US Trenton amphibious landing dock to India. China also disliked the joint naval exercises between Japan, Australia and Singapore in September 2008.
- China and India, despite all agreements, are rivals for energy and water. This has been apparent in Myanmar, where China has built up trade and in Central Asia where India has been trying to establish more energy supplies. China's plans to divert water in Tibet are a threat to the source of India's major rivers.
- China's influence in Myanmar, Bangladesh, Iran, Pakistan and Sri Lanka is seen as an encirclement of India. India's influence in Afghanistan and Central Asia and its increasing links with Thailand, Vietnam, Indonesia, Japan and Australia is seen as a means of preventing the growth of China.
- There is a mounting concern over the growing economic relationship between Nepal and China, and the escalating ignorance of human rights and fundamental freedoms of Tibetan refugees there.
- India has been concerned about growing links between China and Pakistan since 1992, particularly in terms of China's support of Pakistan's nuclear programme and the Chinese support for nuclear reactors at Chashma in the Punjab.
- India's military developments and its increasing international prominence and economic growth have changed the relations between India and China.

Aid to Learning

1. Read the section again on India's relations with China. List as many reasons as you can to support why you think relations may improve. Put each reason on a separate card. Put the cards in the order of importance.
2. List as many reasons as you can about why relations may be difficult. Put each reason on a separate card. Put the cards in the order of importance.

Activities

Role play: It is your job to brief an Indian diplomat being posted to Beijing on the main problems and the main hopes for peace and cooperation between India and Pakistan.

Write your briefing on one side of a sheet of A4 paper (diplomats are busy people and need clear, brief advice).

Aid to Learning

Study the following article and answer the following questions.
1. What do you understand by the cartoon in this article?
2. Why do you think that the region has been 'one of the most militarized in the world'?
3. Why do you think India has invested so much in this submarine?
4. How do you think India's foreign policy makers before 1989 would have reacted to this development?
5. What do you think Indian policy should do to avoid the threat of arms races, conflict and war over the next ten years?
6. What do you think are the major obstacles to peace?

Nuclear Arms Race Heats Up with Launch of India's Nuclear Submarine

The launch of a nuclear submarine will cause an increase in the arms race between India and its neighbours like Pakistan and China and will only add to the instability of the region.

New Delhi, India – Pakistan has stated that India's launch of a nuclear submarine is a threat to regional peace and stability in South Asia.

The Foreign office spokesman Abdul Basit stated that "Pakistan will take appropriate steps to safeguard its security without entering an arms race."

The submarine, unveiled at a ceremony on Sunday, will be able to launch nuclear missiles at targets close to 500 miles away. At Sunday's launch, Prime Minister Manmohan Singh said India had no aggressive designs on anyone. However Pakistan, India's arch-rival, a fellow nuclear power, and a country that has fought three wars with India in the last 60 years, certainly feels threatened.

With the launch of the submarine, India has become only the sixth country in the world to build its own nuclear-powered submarine, until now only the US, Russia, France, Britain and China had the capability to manufacture its own nuclear subs. Till now, India had relied on Russian made submarines for its fleet.

The 6 000 ton Arihant will be deployed in a few years after trials and testing. The Hindi meaning of Arihant is "destroyer of enemies." Up till now, India has been capable of launching missiles only by air and land with its army and air force.

Now the ability to launch nuclear missiles and weapons by sea gives it a triple dimension to its already impressive armed forces in the region. The submarine will have the ability to carry up to 100 sailors on board and will have the capability to stay underwater for long periods of time, making it harder to detect. Analysts believe that the Indian government is looking to not only have an upper hand against Pakistan by having nuclear submarines that the Pakistanis do not possess, but also are attempting to thwart any threats from China which has a huge major naval presence in the Indian and Pacific Oceans.

Nonetheless, the launching of the Indian nuclear submarine will only make an already nervous Pakistan do everything in its power to also either purchase submarines from China, Germany, France or other countries or perhaps start its own long term plans of keeping pace with India by developing its own nuclear submarines with or without assistance from its arms suppliers.

The region does not need a build-up and an increase in the nuclear arms race and one hopes that the two countries focus on diplomacy and a stalled peace process rather than arming themselves to the teeth. The region already is one of the most militarized in the world with three of the world's exclusive nuclear club countries side by side with each other in Pakistan, India and China.

Source: http://www.allvoices.com/contributed-news/3788088-india-nuclear-submarine-munir-heats - the Pakistanis for peace website/ This is an article by ManzerMuinir July 2009

Exercise

1. What is the importance of India's Look East policy?
2. What is the significance of international organisations such as ASEAN for India?
3. Why are relations with China so important for India today?
4. Why are nuclear weapons so important in Indian foreign relations today?
5. Which of the outstanding issues in Indian foreign policy do you think are the most important?

Chapter 15

Relations with USA

Key Question

Why have some Indian governments promoted nuclearisation and with what consequences?

In 1980, India's Foreign Minister described India's relations with the US as 'five wasted decades'. Under Nehru, India had pursued economic policies which were closer to those of the USSR than to the free market system of the US. It protected the Indian industry with tariffs which the US disapproved of. Nehru's hopes for non-aligned nations to form a third force between the opposing sides of the Cold War received little sympathetic response in the US. The turning point was the two wars waged by India in the 1960s against China and Pakistan. India sought and gained military aid from the USSR, which worried the US. The USA hence sought closer ties with Pakistan.

The End of the Cold War

With the collapse of the Soviet Union, the Cold War came to a dramatic end and the whole context changed. India could no longer rely on Russia as its 'superpower' ally. In fact, Russian power started looking distinctly limited by 1991. It was hence not sensible to be on bad terms with the other superpower, while India was having on-going disputes with Pakistan and China. Moreover, the economic modernisation brought India much more in line with the Western economics. India began to make more efforts to reverse its anti-American stance. America, in turn, grew more prepared to have friendly links with a power threatened by Islamic insurgency and which might be a counter-weight to China. The latter's economic and military growth was seen increasingly as a source of concern to US interests.

There were encouraging signs of US-Indian friendship until India's underground nuclear tests at Pokhran in 1999. Sanctions were imposed and India was not allowed to import nuclear technology. Pressure was put on India by restricting loans for non-humanitarian purposes. However, the US did not give Pakistan support in the Kargil War of 1999 and its relations with India did not also revert to the way they were in the 1970s.

Some Significant Changes

- The Clinton administration (1993–2001) gave way to that of George W. Bush whose advisers were more concerned about the power of China.
- The 9/11 terrorist attack in New York in 2001 brought immediate offers of help from India and signalled a new cooperation between the two countries. It also increased US concerns about the 'war on terror' and for allies against Islamic extremism. The US needed Pakistan, but had decided to treat India and Pakistan separately, rather than seeing one as an ally to the exclusion of the other.
- The US wanted the freedom to develop its missile defence system and was less concerned with restricting the options of its overseas friends.
- India had been prepared to be on better terms with Israel since the 1990s. Its foreign policy was based much less on vague moral statements about great colonial powers and the need for Third World aid. Instead, it was based more on practical issues. This accorded more with the US view making it a country with which the US could do business.
- The success of Indian economy, its high growth rates, its modernisation and its links with Asia had made it a more attractive ally.
- The Indian diaspora – the high number of Indians living worldwide – came to include two million in the US. There were effective pro-Indian pressure groups and voters in the USA. The American public was, in general, quite aware of the Indian culture.
- There was an increase in the internal instability of Pakistan. The sympathy of the US for the victims of the terrorist attacks in Kashmir and in India as a whole became stronger.
- The greatly increased trade between India and Europe doubled in the late 1990s and there were much stronger relationships with Israel, one of the strongest allies of the US.

Nehru had favoured close relations with the Arab World. But it was after 1991 that the Indian governments grew closer to Israel. In 1992, India set up full diplomatic relations with Israel for the first time. By 2008, Israel had become a significant trading partner and supplier of military weapons to India. Between 2002 and 2008, India bought $5 billion worth of equipment from Israel and the two countries have been cooperating on spy satellites as well.

Key Elements of US-Indian Relationship

- The ending of sanctions and support for India as a nuclear power.
- Joint military cooperation and naval exercises.
- US corporations supplying India with key military equipment.

- US and India sealing nuclear accord under which India agreed to separate its civil and military nuclear facilities and the US agreed to work towards full civil nuclear cooperation.
- US and India finalising a controversial nuclear deal after talks in Delhi between US President George Bush and the Indian Prime Minister Manmohan Singh, whereby India got access to US civil nuclear technology and its nuclear facilities for inspection – a deal called 'historic' by Bush.
- Ending years of Indian isolation over the nuclear issue.

Fig. 4.9 Condoleezza Rice, the US Secretary of State, with Indian Foreign Minister Pranab Mukherjee, October, 2008.

The Issue of Nuclear Power

Indian nuclear power development goes back to 1957 with the establishment of the Bhabha Atomic Research Centre at Trombay. India did not sign the Nuclear Non-Proliferation Treaty which originated in 1968 against the spread of nuclear weapons. In 1974, it tested its first nuclear weapon. Nuclear development, both civil and military, was difficult because of the restrictions placed on the export of nuclear technology and materials by the Nuclear Suppliers Group of nations formed in 1974. It was also made difficult by the restrictions placed on the US governments by Article 123 of the US Atomic Energy Research Act of 1954 which insisted on strict conditions before the US co-operated with any other nations.

As India refused to sign the Nuclear Non-proliferation Treaty and despite India's commitment to 'no first use' of nuclear weapons, there was every reason to fear a nuclear war between India and Pakistan. The other nations and especially the US were unwilling to assist in the development of Indian nuclear power.

India conducted underground nuclear weapons tests at Pokhran (Operation Shakhti) in April and May 1998 after developing thermonuclear devices in the 1990s. In this, technical assistance had been given by Russia. There was widespread condemnation, especially from the Clinton administration in the US. India was isolated and it seemed unlikely that it would get any cooperation in developing its civil use of nuclear power. In the early years of this century, a shortage of uranium curtailed nuclear energy generation in India quite significantly. Thus, the changing relations with the US from 2001 are extremely significant in that they have seen the US support for a relaxation of restrictions.

To overcome the US domestic legislation, a special act was passed in 2006 through the Congress called the Henry J. Hyde Peaceful Cooperation with India Bill, following talks between the Bush administration and India in 2005. The bill finally became a law in October 2008 and cooperation agreements under Article 123 of the 1954 Act followed. In September 2008, the Nuclear Suppliers Group agreed to waive restrictions on the import of nuclear supplies even though India had not signed the Nuclear Non-Proliferation Treaty, with China reluctant to agree, but with the US supporting strongly. Since the autumn of 2008, India has signed agreements with a number of countries, principally Russia which agreed to supply 2000 tons of nuclear fuel. In addition, Kazakhstan, France and the US have agreed to supply, as have Canada and the UK.

Case Study

India plans to start Russian-built nuclear plant soon

India plans to start up a Russian-built nuclear power plant within weeks, Prime Minister Manmohan Singh says. After talks in Moscow with Russian President Dmitry Medvedev, whose country is eager to build more nuclear power plants abroad, Singh said the first two reactors at the Kudankulam plant were close to being activated.

The power station in the southern state of Tamil Nadu is one of several planned power projects that are seen as vital to plugging huge electricity shortages that have damaged economic growth. However, protests by local people against the power station gathered pace after the Fukushima accident in Japan in March. "We are confident that we will be able to persuade some of these people that their concerns are adequately taken care of, that our nuclear plants are safe and sound and there is nothing to worry about with regards

Fig. 4.10   Manmohan Singh and Russia's President Dmitry Medvedev

to their safety," Singh said. "I am therefore confident that in a couple of weeks we should be able to go ahead with operationalising Kudankulam, and thereafter, by a period of six months, Kudankulam 2," he further added.

The two countries have been in talks to build two more reactors at Kudankulam. Russia's Itar-Tass news agency cited the head of state nuclear power firm Rosatom, Sergei Kiriyenko, as saying Russia would provide India with a multi-billion dollar loan for the project, though no agreement was signed on Friday. Russia is keen to exploit its nuclear know-how, having already built two reactors in China and one in Iran that was plugged into the network in September.

Source: By Rachael Fergusson (Engineering and Technology Magazine) http://eandt.theiet. org/news/2011/dec/india-russia.cfm

Aid to Learning

1. What does the article from a British magazine on p 157 suggest about the importance of the nuclear issue for India's foreign relations?
2. Consider why US-Indian relations have improved. Draw up a poster with a number of reasons in boxes.

There are links between the developments in nuclear power and the following factors.
- India's economic and technological progress since 1991
- Its continuing fears of China and Pakistan
- Its desire to be a strong South and Southeast Asian regional power
- Its concerns for energy supplies
- Its improved relations with the US since 2000
- Its programme of increased defence spending.

Activities

Try and show the above links in a diagram. Before that, different groups in the class should write a little about each of the above factors. Only after that, make a physical link using a piece of string with another group representing another feature. You might eventually create an interesting pattern. Plot this pattern on paper as well.

Conclusion

Greater power brings greater responsibility. One example is the influx of refugees from Bangladesh into the Northeastern region of India. This brings home the need for global solutions to major problems and not just 'globalisation' in the sense of India trying to trade with more countries. Though India's trade with China has grown from $4.8 billion in 2002 to $38 billion in 2008, this has not brought an end to long-standing disputes. As both countries have expanded their armed forces considerably and have come to possess nuclear weapons, this is a great challenge for the leaders of the country. However, defence experts see India's forces as being a decade behind those of China. This is significant as the opportunities for clashes over influence in Asia have expanded considerably subsequent to India's 'Look East Policy'.

India has a lot of regional problems and faces continuing hostility from elements in Pakistan. India faces many internal disruptions as well. For example, 500 people were killed in Kashmir in a so-called proxy war with Pakistan.

1000 died in the northeastern border region. In Central India, 600 were killed in a clash with Maoist rebels. 'Caste crimes' account for 27 000 deaths. Foreign-based terrorism is an on-going problem. Outrages put a lot of pressure on Indian governments to take action against the neighbouring states. However, as a potential power with rising influence in Asia, India is also expected to act responsibly and find long-term solutions to the causes behind terrorism and regional unrest.

India has been highly successful in being granted access to nuclear technology and materials without signing the restrictive Nuclear Non-Proliferation Treaty. However, this has rested on a pro-US policy which is not universally accepted in India. India has gained from making agreements with a whole range of countries.

However, this has meant turning a blind eye to many other issues. For example, in Myanmar, its deals with the military Junta have been criticised. These issues also include ignoring China's human rights record, particularly in Tibet, while negotiating with the Communist leaders. They pertain also to Israel, Putin's Russia and Chechnya. Unlike China, India is a democracy with a free press and opposition parties and it is not always easy to pursue national interests which involve decisions of contested morality.

Exercise

1. What changes have taken place to 'redefine' India's role in the world since 1989? Explain with reference to the following.
   (a) India's relations with Southeast Asia
   (b) India's relations with the USA
   (c) India's relations with China
2. What has changed and what has remained the same in India's relations with Pakistan?
3. What have been the major developments in India as a nuclear power?
4. How important have India's changing relations with Israel been?
5. In groups, take one aspect each of the following and suggest how India should act in the future.
   (a) How should India develop her influence over international organisations such as ASEAN?
   (b) What should India do about Kashmir and its relations with Pakistan?
   (c) How should India ensure the friendship of the USA?
   (d) What should India's policy be if it becomes one of the permanent members of the Security Council of the UN?
   (e) What policy should India take towards nuclear weapons?

Acknowledgements

We would like to thank the following for permission to use their material in either the original or adapted form:

Institute of Conflict Management (South Asia Terrorism Portal); Global Trade Information Services, Inc.; Pakistanisforpeace.com; South India Cell for Human Rights Education and Monitoring; www.headlinesindia.mapsofindia.com

Credits for Maps, figures and tables

p. 6 Table 1.1 from www.Indian-elections.com/india-statistics.html; p.12 Table 1.2 from Election Commission of India (nethelper.com/article/Elections in_India); p. 14 Fig. 1.4 from http://www.sikhiwiki.org/index.php/File:Blue_star_akal_takht.jpg; p. 19 Fig. 1.5 from http://www.businessweek.com/globalbiz/content/jan2008/gb20080115_921713. htm; p. 26 Fig. 1.6 from http://en.wikipedia.org/wiki/File:Laluprasadyadav.jpg; p. 28 Fig. 1.7 from http://www.whitefl agbook.com/2012/04/naxal-group-which-wasdeclared-as. html; p. 33 Fig. 1.8 from http://eci.nic.in/ECI_Main/Audio_VideoClips/gallery-images/ photo-69.jpg; p. 34 Fig. 1.9 from REUTERS/ArkoDatta # photo 21; p. 35 Fig. 1.10 from news.bbc.co.uk/1/hi/in_pictures/7985415.stm; p. 35 Fig. 1.11 from news.bbc.co.uk/1/hi/ in_pictures/7985415.stm; p. 35 Fig. 1.12 from news.bbc.co.uk/1/hi/in_pictures/7985415. stm; p. 41 Table 2.1 from http://india.gov.in/sectors/commerce/india_trade.php; p. 43 Fig. 2.2 from Ministry of Statistics and Programme Implementation; p. 45 Fig. 2.3 from headlinesindia.com; p. 52 Fig. 2.4 from http://aidindia.org/main/content/view/938/407/; p. 54 Fig. 2.5 image courtesy of Wikipedia; p. 58 Fig. 2.6 from http://upload.wikimedia. org/wikipedia/commons/9/9d/Growth_of_number_of_employees_of_New_Private_ Sector_Banks_in_India.png; p. 58 Fig. 2.7 from http://www.citehr.com/187004-freedom-midnight-speech-jawaharlalnehru.html; p. 67 Fig. 2.10 from Economic Survey 2011–2012; p. 68 Table 2.2 from FDI Intelligence Union Budget 2007–08, RBI Monthly Bulletin, Annual Report & Weekly Statistical Supplement, Ministry of Finance, Ministry of Commerce and Industry, CSO, Institute of international Finance (IIF), ERU NASSCOM; p. 69 Fig. 2.11 from http://www.nistads.res.in/indiasnt2008/images/it4industry/t4ind14_ Fig1.jpg; p. 70 Fig. 2.12 from http://www.nistads.res.in/indiasnt2008/images/it4industry/ t4ind6_Fig4.jpg; p. 71 Fig. 2.13 from http://graphics.thomsonreuters.com/0210/ IN_STL0210.gif; p. 72 Table 2.3 from World Bank, Basic indicators; p. 75 Table 2.4 from

hdrstats.undp.org; p. 75 Table 2.5 from Human Development Report;
p. 76 Fig. 2.14 from undp.org; p. 76 Fig. 2.15 from undp.org; p. 77 Map 2.1 from http://
www.mapsofindia.com/maps/india/poverty.html; p. 79 Fig. 2.16 from http://sichrem.
files.wordpress.com/2010/07/image007.jpg; p. 82 Fig. 2.19 image courtesy of Wikipedia;
p. 87 Fig. 3.1 from http://nicsr.in/wpcontent/uploads/2011/02/14.jpg; p. 89 Table 3.1
from Government of India, Time Use Survey, 1998–1999; p. 91 Fig. 3.4 from http://
archive.unu.edu/unupress/food/8F114e/8F114E02.gif; p. 92 Map 3.1 from http://
dillipost.in/wp-content/uploads/2011/05/Change-of-child-Sex-ratio-map-2001-2011-
india.jpg; p. 93 Fig. 3.5 from http://www.shsu.edu/~eco_hkn/dowry.jpg; p. 96 Fig. 3.6
from http://shwarnimsavera.com/images/730px-Literacy_Bar_Chart.jpg; p. 96 Fig. 3.7
from http://daily.bhaskar.com/article/; p. 101 Fig. 3.10 from http://upload.wikimedia.
org/wikipedia/en/0/08/1990,_August,_31,_Road_block_for_Mandal_Commission_
protest,_Chandigarh,_India.jpg; p. 105 Fig. 3.12 from http://progressivemedialeap.
files.wordpress.com/2011/01/mid-day-meal-2.jpg; p. 114 Fig. 3.15 from http://www.
oktatabyebye.com/TravelBlog-images/IMG_6178.JPG; p. 116 Fig 3.18 from en.wikipedia.
org/wiki/file:Ahmedabad_riot01.jpg; p. 117 Fig. 3.19 from http://www.livemint.com/
articles/48ca70fa-cbac-11df-b185-000b5dabf613_39_39SubVPF.gif; p. 120 Fig. 3.20
from www.sinlung.com/2001/03/delhisays-no-tribals.html; p. 125 Fig. 4.1 from http://
newshopper.sulekha.com/manmohan-singh-abhisitvejjajiva_photo_1026308.htm; p. 131
Fig. 4.3 image courtesy Wikipedia; p. 135 Map 4.1 courtesy Wikipedia; p. 136 Fig. 4.4
image courtesy Wikipedia; p.137 Fig. 4.5 from Press Information Bureau; p. 138
Fig. 4.6 from http://islamicseminary.org/Upload/634039469791193640_051102N1_0R28
P.jpg; p. 141 Fig. 4.7 from http://www.diplomacywatch.com/news-stories2.php?id=106; p.
143 Map 4.3 courtesy Wikipedia; p. 144 Map 4.4 courtesy Wikipedia; p. 146 Fig. 4.8 from
Global Trade Atlas; p. 148 Map 4.5 courtesy Wikipedia; p. 156 Fig. 4.9 image courtesy
Wikipedia; p. 157 Fig. 4.10 image courtesy Wikipedia.

Every effort has been made to ensure that website addresses are correct at the time of
going to press. However, the publisher cannot be held responsible for the content of any
website mentioned in this book.

Index